POPULATIONS IN DANGER

POPULATIONS IN DANGER

Médecins Sans Frontières

Edited by François Jean

John Libbey
JL
LONDON · PARIS · ROME

British Library Cataloguing in Publication Data

Populations in Danger
    I. Jean, François
ISBN: 0 86196 392 X

This work is the English translation of the original work in the French langauge
Populations en Danger, edited by François Jean, published in Paris by Hachette.

Published by

John Libbey & Company Ltd, 13 Smiths Yard, Summerley Street,
London SW18 4HR, England
Telephone: 081-947 2777 – Fax: 081-947 2664
John Libbey Eurotext Ltd, 6 rue Blanche, 92120 Montrouge, France
John Libbey - C.I.C. s.r.l., via Lazzaro Spallanzani 11, 00161 Rome, Italy

Printed in Great Britain by Whitstable Litho Ltd, Whitstable, Kent, U.K.

Contents

Authors and acknowledgements

Authors

Part One:

Colette Braeckman, Alain Destexhe, Odile Hardy, Guy Hermet, François Jean, Alain Labrousse, Bertil Lintner, Roland Marchal, Eric Meyer, Roland-Pierre Paringaux, Gérard Prunier, Michel Sailhan, Antoine Sfeir, Brigitte Silberstein, Marie-Pierre Subtil, Claire Trean, Charles Urjewicz, Mathieu Verboud.

Part Two:

Philippe Biberson, Rony Brauman, Alain Destexhe, Guy Hermet, François Jean, Jean-Christophe Rufin, Jean Rigal, Françoise Bouchet-Saulnier, all of *Médecins Sans Frontières*.

Research and information

Jessica Barry, Bernard Chomillier, Jacques de Milliano, Anne Fouchard, Luc Frejacques, Anne-Marie Huby, Michel Kassa, Odile Marie, Jean-Luc Nahel, Christophe Paquet, Dominique Rousset and Françoise Bouchet-Saulnier with Anne Guibert and Fabrice Weissman.

English transalation

Nora Fitzsimmons, Timothy Fox, Alison Marschner, Pauline Ridel and Gillian Xeridat. Edited by Anne-Marie Huby.

We should also like to thank Reginald Moreels, Rony Brauman, Jacques de Milliano, Pierre Harze and Paul Vermeulen for their advice and comments. We give special thanks to all representatives and volunteers of *Médecins Sans Frontières* in the field for their precious information and support.

PART ONE

INTRODUCTION

As front-seat witnesses to the major world crises over the past 20 years, Médecins Sans Frontières volunteers are also players on the only team that resists the wear and tear of ideologies, i.e. the solidarity team. Yet in a world of almost constant upheaval where news stories vie for sensational headline space, there is a very real risk that compassion might dissolve in the acid of fatalism, weariness and oblivion. The ambition of this book is to confront such a danger by giving a concise glimpse of the context of today's most serious crises in order to emphasize – beyond statistical analyses and strategic considerations – the human element. Conflicts, floods of refugees, under-development, famines, epidemics, demographic explosion: the day-to-day coverage of such crises, by mixing up human tragedy and social facts, true accounts and alarmist cliches, has blurred understanding of the 'Third World' so much that it increasingly appears to be locked behind the bars of pity, aid, paternalism and fear.

We strongly believe that better understanding will lead to resolving this restricted vision. We are convinced that our extensive experience in the field, our determination to understand and our freedom of judgement and speech will allow us to contribute to this in a special way. That is why, with the exception of an article laying out the principles and constraints of crisis medicine, the operations of MSF and other humanitarian organizations are not reviewed here. Neither an in-house plea nor a report of our activities, this book is an appeal for mobilizing the intelligence and the determination to understand as much as the capacity to be outraged and take action. By avoiding present trends and fads in the hope of preventing the tragedy of silence from being added to that of violence, this testimony is part of the humanitarian commitment.

Such an undertaking is open to two main dangers: an ethnic bias, in which conflicts invariably trade in tribal 'identity', and a misery bias that leads to drawing up an endless list of the world's suffering and oppressed. To avoid this double minefield, we have decided to spotlight populations in danger, rather than peoples or tribes, by placing ethnic identity as one of many other elements in an often broader picture. Deliberately avoiding any attempt at exhaustiveness, we have chosen a limited number of situations which appear to us as the most critical: the evolving nature of the crises and the existence of a degree of gravity determine this choice.

For this report – the first in a series aimed at taking these changes into account and bearing witness to tragedies that have been overlooked – is deliberately limited to the 10 cases that seem to us the most serious in the past year. They are basically characterized by the existence of conflicts or internal strife, by population displacement caused by political turmoil and, for some, by the presence of famine or epidemics in very tense contexts.

Our criteria

In other words the 'danger' mentioned in the book's title is the danger of death, the very thing we struggle with on a daily basis. 'Unnatural' death, caused by a curable disease or a treatable wound, by an epidemic that a vaccine could have stopped, this kind of death is a black mark for humankind and a failure for the doctor. But as mortality varies both in its intensity and its causes, when translated into statistics it is the key indicator of the degree of gravity as used by medical organizations to direct initial actions and then adapt their work to the situation's evolution. Violent death is often followed by slower death, caused by epidemic disease – measles, meningitis, cholera, diarrhoea and respiratory infections – or famine.

The purely medical criterion of gravity is not enough to assess the hierarchy of emergencies and crises. There is another one, of a more social nature, which is the precariousness caused by displacement of population. Such movements, triggered by war and famine, plunge whole populations into the most extreme material deprivation and, undoubtedly even more seriously, into a profound psychological distress that makes already weakened bodies more vulnerable. This is why, beyond the supply of shelter, water, food and medical care, moral comfort, 'immaterial aid', provided by the very presence of aid workers, constitutes primary aid, and not simply on the symbolic level.

Ten populations have been chosen to feature in this document because they face imminent – and often measurable – life-threatening danger, best defined by the two criteria above. As a result some situations of real gravity have not been included, even though they have serious ethical, political and sociological implications. This initial bias has led us to leave out, among others, the 'new poor' of the industrialized countries, the Palestinians, the Haitians and the Tibetans, although some of their problems are cited in the second section of this report.

The ten situations

Although there is no such thing as a 'compassion protocol' allowing us to organize the 10 situations into a hierarchy of misery, Sudan undeniably has the sinister privilege of winning the gold medal for horror. More racial than religious, the conflict here involves a veritable process of extermination that the rare and timid reactions of the international community do nothing to disturb. There is no room here for humanitarian action, other than acting as an impotent witness to the massive deportations of southern refugees from Khartoum or to bloody advances on various fronts. There is nothing to indicate that pressure from the international community would stop the process, but it is clear that nothing is being done even to try. For the hundreds of thousands of victims of this ideological carnage, the 'world order' remains one of indifference and non-assistance to a population in danger of extermination. Although very late in the day, Somalia now draws more international attention than Sudan, even if it is not receiving the star billing of Ethopia in 1984. The joint effects of war and drought have brought a devastating famine, made all the more deadly by the armed gangs and warlords who jeopardize the safe delivery of humanitarian aid. But at least humanitarian aid is possible in Somalia, even if there is great risk for aid volunteers and right of passage is paid dearly. This has only lately been true in the war zones of the former Yugoslavia where relief operations were either forbidden or targeted for attack in the first months of the conflict. Yet there is no reason to be happy about the charitable international mobilization that followed President Mitterrand's trip to Sarajevo on June 28, 1992. For humanitarian aid was limited to the role of a mere travelling companion to a strategy of territorial conquest and 'ethnic cleansing' that we would have liked to believe had been banished from Europe. On top of more than 40,000 deaths, the two million refugees are not a consequence but a goal of this war, with the resurgence of concentration camps as the temporary result, the basic lesson of which might serve other apprentice dictators in Europe: whatever the degree of savagery or the nature of political objectives, you can get away with anything as long as a few humanitarian convoys are allowed to get through.

As if the endless war raging in Mozambique were not enough, a new drought has hit the countryside, creating pockets of famine in areas where violence prohibits the delivery of aid. The main problem here, as in a number of other conflicts in the world, is the lack both of access to victims and of control over aid. These crucial questions will not be solved unless donor governments and organizations assert their determination to ensure both the freedom of the aid agencies to assess needs and their right to control aid delivery. These are the intangible fundamentals of this new right of humanitarian assistance that is now being created. With such clear support from their donor governments, organizations in the field would gain greater room for manoeuvre and negotiation in their daily activities. It would then be up to them to prove their operational abilities and their determination to respect – and have respected – the responsibilities incumbent on humanitarian agencies. Reducing misappropriations in itself justifies the introduction of such control. More fundamentally, it is vital for food aid not to become a fearful weapon in the hands of political powers, a new means of oppression rather than a vital act of solidarity.

Not unlike Yugoslavia, massive expulsion of population by any possible means is also the political objective of the Burmese government, which intends to chase out of the country one of the groups that make up the complex mosaic of ethnic and religious groups in Burma. Here the victims are the Rohingyas, Burmese Moslems, considered by Rangoon as immigrants and once again used as scapegoats. Flattened villages, rapes, beatings and executions: the litany of terror remains horrifically familiar. The gang in power remains firmly entrenched despite a 90 per cent vote against it in the last elections. The United States and Europe have repeatedly condemned Burma but their outrage has not stopped American and European companies from maintaining lucrative business relations with Rangoon, thus allowing one of the world's most corrupt and repressive regimes to stay in power.

In Sri Lanka on the other hand, the democratically elected government lives on despite a civil war that is almost 10 years old. The paradoxical consequence of this unexpected and incomplete victory of the rule of law is that the war against the Tamils continues and the democratic principles proclaimed by the government at the same time as it violates them are wearing thin. Trapped between the hammer of the Sri Lankan army and the anvil of the Tamil 'Tigers', the civilian population in the war zones is paying an enormous price.

Even more difficult to solve are the problems of the Shining Path guerrilla movement and the omnipresence of drug traffickers which are together driving Peru year by year deeper into economic chaos and social violence. Its main victims are the Indian popu-lations. It should surprise no one that in a context of economic paralysis and massive rural exodus cholera has spread so quickly and taken such a heavy toll.

The Tuaregs, other guardians of tradition, politically rejected and turned into social outcasts, have risen in revolt. First forced into a resettlement allegedly justified by the imposition of frontiers and technocratic imperatives of 'development', victims of a his-toric revenge against former slave traders, they have been sucked into a spiral of violence and repression that has thrown more than 120,000 of them into exile and life in refugee camps in Algeria and Mauritania.

If few of the situations already mentioned have been widely reported in the news, such is not the case of the Kurds of Iraq whose suffering was seen live on our television screens. The prospect of a regional quagmire and the emotion of public opinion caused the Kurdish exodus of April 1992 to unleash an unprecedented military and humani-tarian operation which soon reached its main objective: making these bothersome refugees return home as quickly as possible under Allied protection. A year and a half afterwards, as the Western air cover based in Turkey is about to be withdrawn and the protocol for humanitarian aid between the UN and the Iraqi government comes to an end, the Kurds are struck by a double blockade: by the Allies against Baghdad and by Baghdad against them. Threatened, harassed and attacked by the Iraqi gov-ernment, humanitarian organizations have had to reduce their personnel and, in some cases, even leave the area. Baghdad intends to get rid of embarrassing witnesses, for as everyone in Iraq knows, the Kurds' fate depends on their ability to rally international opinion. Above and beyond the Kurdish question, the main cause for concern remains Saddam Hussein's implacable dictatorship, yet again evident in his ruthless repression of the Shia Moslems in the south. Yet not long ago he was considered the Western countries' steadfast ally against the Islamic threat and armed to the hilt by the super-powers and their allies. He was even saved in extremis by them to preserve regional stability. Today he has become the West's scapegoat for its own political impotence.

Far from the limelight, the conflicts that are bloodying the Caucasus, especially embar-rassing for the European countries, are apt symbols of the end of the Soviet empire. With thousands of casualties, hundreds of thousands of refugees, the economic col-lapse of Armenia and Azerbaijan, utter confusion and immense frustration, everything is in place for would-be despots to crush the last hopes of the region's fledgling democ-racies.

As a new social phenomenon and a fully-fledged player in the international system, working in a world that has been made freer but more complex by the disintegration of communism, the humanitarian movement must now add specific reflection to the obvious fact of action.

First, let us hazard a minimum definition. Humanitarian action aims to preserve life and human dignity and to restore people's ability to choose. To accept such a definition is to say that in contrast to other areas of international solidarity, humanitarian aid does not aim to transform society but to help its members get through a crisis period, in other words when there has been a break with a previous balance. To add that humanitarian aid is implemented peacefully and without discrimination by independent and impartial organizations is to set both the shape of the stage and the outlines of the actors. This definition especially affirms the special status of private humanitarian organizations in contrast to governments exercising a new role in the humanitarian field. Invoking the 'principles of humanity, the demands of public conscience, and jus gentium', to use the deliberately generic yet precise terms of the Geneva Conventions, is to enshrine this action in humanistic ethics. Contrary to the political world, the motivation is para-mount where aid organizations are concerned, as important as the very results of the action. The space for humanitarian aid is thereby indicated by three markers:

1. Motivation. Humanitarian aid should be guided by concern for others, not the defence of interests. Would the marketing of medical services, even if their usefulness were not doubted, be considered humanitarian? Or the sending of aid exclusively to the Moslems of Bosnia by Turkish Moslems ? Or the creation by the Nazis in 1933 of Winterhilfe, an aid agency for the 'Aryan' victims of the Great Depression in Germany? Whatever the benefit for the recipients of such aid, it is plain that business interests or religious, ethnic and ideological solidarity cannot ever be called humanitarian.

2. The context in which the act is carried out, i.e. the harsh break with a previous balance. It is a vague, imperfect notion but useful for keeping us from setting our own standards as universally valid. It is in a crisis environment – be it of natural or political

origin, an earthquake or a civil war – that humanitarian action takes on its full meaning. In helping individuals and groups through a harsh period until they can regain their autonomy, humanitarian aid is radically different from developmental aid, which urges a deliberate transformation of lifestyle.

3. Independence. Unequivocally there must be independence from all political powers. Especially in time of war, the part played by humanitarian agencies must be totally clear. In a climate that is by definition very tense, it is in fact the very condition required to establish an atmosphere of trust, without which restrictions on movement and fears for the safety of aid workers stop any effective humanitarian action. Of course there is no deed of property for this territory but the three attributes above mark out humanitarian work in contrast with other areas of solidarity.

The second part of this report gives perspective to the human problems raised by the first part. Conflicts have gone through a character change with the disappearance of East-West tension. The United States and the Soviet Union used to guarantee, for better or for worse, a kind of regulation that has now vanished. The appearance of confirmed regional powers, like India and China, and new minor players – Pakistan, Iran, Libya, Iraq and Israel – on the scene of internal and regional conflicts has made the international game highly unpredictable. Since the right of veto in the Security Council was put on hold, the UN has been trying to realize its founding dream of marrying the dynamics of peace with those of solidarity. This ambitious goal deserves praise, but it will force the UN to redefine the mandates of its agencies so that activities of political mediation and humanitarian aid coordination stop weakening each other, as is the case in Somalia, Bosnia and Iraq.

Likewise the notion of refugee will have to be revised, for there are different definitions today that can have contradictory consequences. In fact, there are three categories of refugee: those who flee war or internal upheaval by crossing a border, those who flee for the same reasons but seek shelter in another part of their own country, and those who want to escape political, religious or ethnic persecution. Only the first and third have the right to the 'refugee' label, the second group being qualified as 'displaced persons'. Why not distinguish between war refugees, whether or not they leave their home countries, and political refugees? The first would receive the aid and protection provided for in the Geneva Conventions for the duration of the conflict. The second could be relocated in another country and enjoy its social and political rights. It is a distinction easier to make than to put into effect, of course, but closer to reality and more likely to respond to the basic needs of refugees. The appearance of war refugees in Europe might stimulate the interest of politicians and legislators, which has faded away with the end of the Cold War. In the past the very existence of refugees used to prove the failure of communism, the 'peoples's republics' of the Third World 'producing' nearly 90 per cent of the total number of the world's refugee population. Refugees provided glaring evidence of the enemy's failure; today they are in the way, devoid of ideological or strategic interest, perceived in the light of immigration and of the financial burden that their presence entails.

Almost always in the wake of populations d splaced by war, famines can break out even where there is no noticeable food shortage although they obviously reach maximum scale when the effects of drought are mixed with those of war. Hunger as a means of subduing or reducing the opposition, whatever the cost to civilians, is a classic war weapon that belligerents have never refrained from using. Orchestrated or not, famine is more often due to a break in the food supply chain than to the overall shortage of food. This makes it radically different from chronic malnutrition, which is due to poverty or rather to injustice in wealth distribution in the Third World. This distinction not only sheds another light on famine, it also leads to alternative, and even opposing, solutions. Emergency food aid is necessary in cases of famine whereas it is not advisable, and can even be harmful, in situations of chronic malnutrition for it has a negative effect on local production. The same goes for the treatment of the pathological consequences of malnutrition, which differ according to whether it is acute or chronic.

The rhetoric commonly used in this regard is more often inspired by unrealistic anxieties than by careful analysis. Galloping birth rates are described in apocalyptic terms alongside famines, war and devastation. Yet apart from a few notable exceptions, densely populated countries produce more than they consume, while penury and malnutrition haunt a number of thinly populated countries The equation 'more population = more hunger and poverty = more immigration' owes less in fact to lucid observation than to a Malthusian obsession slapped on to carefully selected situations. Playing on fear, confusing images of famished hordes, destroyed forests and dried lakes, the Green Malthusian rhetoric does a lot to blur understanding.

Having tackled these questions, we must set out to elucidate the effective conditions for action. As a special passport for entering the territory of humanitarian aid, medicine, wherever it is practised, remains medicine. Yet its priorities, its organizational forms, its 'theatre of operations' and, to a degree, its indicators that help guide action are specific. The initial assessment – based on demography, nutritional status, history, local facilities and logistics – is decisive for the action that follows. The attention that the international community can bring to the problem is just as important, for it contributes to giving humanitarian agencies the necessary means – protection, funding and logistics – to carry out quality relief action. This shows further that humanitarian action depends on its ability to appeal to public opinion, and that its very future depends on its credibility and independence. Our most devout wish is that this document will contribute to strengthening these principles.

Médecins Sans Frontières

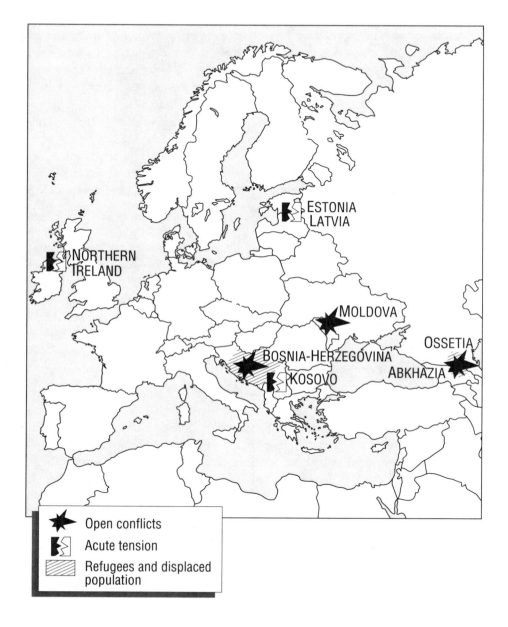

Open conflicts

Acute tension

Refugees and displaced population

EUROPE

Introduction

Terrible sights which we had hoped never to see again have reappeared on the European scene. Throngs of refugees flee bombardments or armed militias. Peoples are hard put to obtain food and are thrust headlong back into economic, social and health care underdevelopment. Communities wake up to find that they are exiles in their own land in the new states of Eastern Europe. The 'new order', the birth of which was heralded on the still-smoking ruins of communism, is struggling to find itself, in pain and insecurity, within the greater Europe.

The collapse of regimes of the soviet type had a liberating effect for the better, but also for the worse. It took the lid off the frustrations built up by peoples who had for too long been dispossessed of their cultural, religious or national identity and it acted as a detonator for their resentment. It also threw into sharp relief the flaws of a collectivist system which had been carefully concealed for decades and – initially, at any rate – accelerated the breakdown of economies. In some cases, all of these factors (economic slump, fear, war) combined to throw on to the roads of Europe populations which had known no such extensive movement since the last world war.

Even in the central European countries, which were in theory the least ill-prepared, the changeover to a market economy was a painful experience. One of the first results of the end of iron control was the disorganization of economies, a drop in production and disruption of the distribution channels. With no real social welfare system, the social cost of reforms is enormous, unpopular and potentially a source of destabilization. It also varies from one region to the next : this disparity and the resulting divergent assessments of the suitable rhythm for reforms were largely responsible, for example, for the break between Czechs and Slovaks.

The situation is even more serious in the former USSR where the overall disorganization of the economy only adds to considerable disparity in the development of different republics or ethnic groups. Thus, infant mortality is four times higher among the Tajiks than among the Baltic population, three times higher among the Turkmens or Kirghiz than among the Ukrainians or Belarussians.

Furthermore, the dislocation of the Soviet Union resulted in the reappearance of a map of nationalities which does not coincide with the administrative boundaries of the former republics. This is an explosive situation. In the former USSR 65 million people are living outside their republic of origin, including 25 million Russians who – in the Baltic States, Moldova or Central Asia – are afraid that they will soon be considered second-class citizens if this is not already the case. Russia is receiving a wave of refugees (the official figure is 280,000 but the number was estimated at three million in mid-1992) which it does not have the means to feed, house or employ.

Nevertheless, all the displaced persons are not Russians. People of all nationalities are fleeing from the regions affected by open or potential civil wars, which are on the increase in the former Soviet Union. A number of such crises, such as that of Nagorno-Karabakh, had broken out even before the central Soviet power collapsed. Dislocation of the 'empire' merely accentuated the tensions between nationalities. The fighting between Moldovans and Russian-speakers calling for the independence of 'Trans-Dniestr' is a sorry illustration of the deadly conflicts which are developing and are in danger of spreading right across the former USSR.

In Yugoslavia, the awakening of nationalistic feeling ushered in the worst possible events. When the time comes to count them, there will be tens of thousands of victims of the 'Greater Serbia' dream which Milosevic and his followers tried to use as a bulwark against the aspirations of the republics towards independence. Horror has gripped the very heart of old Europe, bringing with it practices thought to be banished once and for all from this part of the continent. This is a conflict which turns its back on the most elementary rules of war, with towns and cities taken hostage, civilians held in detention camps, large-scale massacres and the driving out of whole peoples in the name of the 'ethnic cleansing' so dear to the Serbian extremists.

Faced with these catastrophes which far exceed anything forseeen, the European Community protects its boundaries against an influx of refugees, provides financial assistance within the modest limits of what public opinion is likely to tolerate and attempts to hide its powerlessness behind aid projects which cannot distract from its incapacity to put forward political solutions to the situation.

AUSTRIA

HUNGARY

ROMANIA

Slovenia

Ljubljana   • Zagreb

Croatia   Vukovar•

Voivodina

• Novi Sad

Zadar•

*Bosnia-
Herzegovina*

• Belgrade

Split•   • Sarajevo

Serbia

*ADRIATIC
SEA*

Montenegro

Dubrovnik•   Titograd   Pristina •

Kosovo

BULGARIA

• Skopje

ITALY

• Tirana

Macedonia

ALBANIA   GREECE

	Zones occupied by Serbs
	Zones held by Moslems
	Zones held by Croats

THE FORMER YUGOSLAVIA

The most pessimistic scenario has won out in Yugoslavia. Confirming the darkest predictions, the country did not outlive Marshal Tito by more than 10 years. For the civilian population, this is an unending tragedy which is being played out on the European Community's doorstep.

It is necessary to go back to the aftermath of World War II to find upheavals of such gravity on the continent. In July 1992, this conflict had already caused more than 40,000 deaths, tens of thousands of wounded and missing, more than two million people trudging along the roads of exodus, 500,000 of whom are refugees in the neighbouring countries. The displaced populations are not merely the main victims of the fighting, they are also deliberate targets and at the same time both the objective and the stakes in this pitiless conflict. The massacres and the forced transfers of populations, the hostage-taking and the holding of civilians in detention camps all hark back to the 'ethnic cleansing' policy that had been announced since 1986. It was finally carried out as promised in the heart of a Europe reduced to the role of charitable and powerless witness.

Civilian populations in agony: from Vukovar ...

Tito's Yugoslavia was built upon the suppression of the fratricidal memories of 1941–45, on the authoritarian integration of nationalities within a federal framework and on the quenching of nationalistic claims. This fortuitous community worked for more than 40 years before breaking down under the weight of a triple political, economic and nationalist crisis. Once reawakened, the nationalistic spirit rapidly struck an aggressive stance. In 1989, Serbia under Milosevic called Tito's balance into question by nourishing the dream of a 'greater Serbia' and by 'reconquering' Kosovo – 90 per cent of whose inhabitants are Albanians – which lost its independence in 1990. Turmoil and provocations increased until Slovenia and Croatia, by this time convinced that the Federation had no future, proclaimed their independence on 25 June 1991. The federal army, in which most officers were Serbian or Montenegrin, immediately went on the offensive.

After an initial humiliating failure in Slovenia, the army went on to attack Slavonia, a region of Croatia with a mixed population. Before the war, Vukovar was made up of 35 per cent Croats, 30 per cent Serbs and 35 per cent minorities). When the first elections were held in May 1990, Vukovar was one of the rare towns in Croatia to escape the exalted nationalism of Tudjman's party. The siege of the town began on 2 September and lasted three months. It was a horrific ordeal for the 20,000 people who remained, huddled in basements, to be subjected to shelling which did not even spare the hospital, overflowing as it was with the wounded. After three months of intensive bombardment, the town and the surrounding villages were completely destroyed. More than 4500 people, including 2000 civilians, were killed and hundreds of those who escaped death were herded off to detention camps long unheard of by the international community.

In a matter of three months, a wall of hate was thrown up in Croatia and Serbia between communities living side by side. Propaganda escalated to rave about the past crimes of the 'Ustashis' and the 'Chetniks', out-of-control militias abounded, wounds so recently healed reopened, 'mixed' married couples broke up and the younger generations who thought that they were Yugoslavs suddenly discovered that they were 'Serbs' or 'Croats'. Scenes of horror took place on both sides and were answered by reprisals, thus hardening the situation into a spiral of violence.

The conflict in Croatia ended for a time when the UN peacekeepers moved in during February 1992. One third of Croatia is occupied (Slavonia, Baranja, western Srem and Krajina, which has a Serbian majority). These areas have been practically emptied of their non-Serb inhabitants. The situation of the Serbs in Croatia is no better, for most have had to leave the country. Those who insist on staying live in a climate of suspicion and are often treated as second-class citizens. This attempt to standardize populations is also apparent in Vojvodina and in Serbia where the extremists – tolerated, or even encouraged by the regime – put pressure on the non-Serb minorities to encourage them to leave. In Kosovo, which the Serbs consider the cradle of their civilization, the local inhabitants are subjected to a terrorist occupation.

To Sarajevo ...

In April 1992, after its declaration of independence, Bosnia-Herzegovina, where the inhabitants are of particularly mixed origin (44 per cent Moslems, 33 per cent Serbs, 17 per cent Croats), in turn got bogged down in the war. The antagonisms which had

Violations of humanitarian law in the Yugoslav conflict

Fighting in Yugoslavia is marked by systematic violation of the clauses of the Second Protocol of the Geneva Conventions concerning the protection of civilian populations in non-international armed conflicts.

– Article 4 lists as fundamental guarantees : interdiction to order that there should be no survivors, interdiction to murder or engage in cruel or degrading treatment, collective punishments, taking of hostages, etc.

The number of prisoners in this conflict has always been very small. They have often been executed or used for bartering purposes.

The notion of a national group and collective responsibility has taken precedence over the distinction between civilian and combatant. Civilian populations have often been used as a human shield during fighting, as guinea pigs during de-mining operations or for bartering, notably to have a blockade lifted on barracks.

– Article 5 authorizes detention only for persons directly involved in the fighting.

Internment of civilians in the detention camps is in absolute contradiction with the immunity of the civilian population.

– Articles 7 and 12 protect the wounded and ill together with the personnel, units and means of transport marked with the sign of the Red Cross.

From the very start, the belligerents have unlawfully used the Red Cross emblem, particularly for the transport of weapons. On the other hand, all health operations have become targets for direct or indirect strikes and hospitals are regularly bombarded.

– Article 13 forbids acts the main aim of which is to spread terror among the civilian population.

The entire manner in which the conflict is being handled reveals a deliberate strategy aimed at terrorizing the population in order to redraw the ethnic map of the country.

– Article 17 forbids forced movement of populations.

The 'ethnic cleansing' logic is in absolute contradiction with the rules and the spirit of humanitarian law.

had more than enough time to feed on the hate born of the atrocities committed in Croatian territory exploded into a tidal wave of violence. Sarajevo, the capital, where the various communities have been living together for centuries, gives us a sad example of the tragedy of Bosnia-Herzegovina. The city, which is sited in a declivity, is ceaselessly bombarded by the Serbian artillery hidden in the hills. The inhabitants are torn between holding out together against the attackers and following the ethnic divide.

Europe powerless

Throughout the Yugoslav crisis, Europe, apparently powerless, has taken too much time to react and has not managed to prevent the worsening of the situation. Opinions were divided, causing hesitation as to aims and means. Was Yugoslavia to be maintained or were the new republics to be acknowledged ? Should the aggressor be denounced or were the fighting parties to be dismissed unsatisfied? After they recognized Bosnia-Herzegovina's independence, Europe and the United Nations were incapable of protecting it against the aggression which was unleashed in reaction. This powerlessness is also linked to collective blindness concerning the real aims of Serbia.

As a result of all these hesitations, the European Community allowed the conflict to develop and reach unbelievable dimensions. In order to justify its passive attitude and its refusal to intervene, it continually fell back on humanitarian action. This activity was to keep up the illusion of a commitment on the part of Europe and to act as alibi for politicians struck down with paralysis. Humanitarian activism, practised at the highest level, only partially hid the incapacity to take the smallest political initiative likely to provide a solution to the conflict. Thus Serbia and its militias were able to apply fully their 'ethnic cleansing' project without the least dissuasive threat. The 'new world order' and 'the right to intervene' died somewhere along the road from Vukovar to Sarajevo.

This humanitarian consensus is not without ambiguity. Faced with the greatest exodus since World War II, Europe is using all the means in its power to hold back the tide of refugees fleeing from the territory of former Yugoslavia. In Bosnia, humanitarian aid masks the lack of political commitment, but politics spring to the fore again as soon as something as serious as immigration has to be dealt with. The United Nations High Commissioner for Refugees was obliged to remind those concerned that 'ethnic cleansing' could not be used as an alibi for further evasion: admission and protection, if only temporary, should be granted to all those who need it.

The entire republic is affected by the fighting. The Bosnian leaders no longer have any control over the situation, the militia are steadily increasing in number and all of them perpetrate atrocities on the inhabitants. However, the apparent symmetry of the massacres should not hide the political mainspring behind this grim escalation of horror. Backed by the federal army, the Serbian extremists are on all fronts applying a policy of 'ethnic cleansing' which, in a word, means terror: maverick bombardments to cause civilians to flee, destruction of non-Serb villages and Moslem districts, massacres and forced transfers of the population. These population-moving operations are not merely the consequence of the war, they are the very objective of the conflict. The aim is to redraw the borders by carving up this multinational republic and set up homogeneous enclaves interlinked by military occupation, terror and the exodus of the 'undesirable' elements. Milosevic's followers claim 70 per cent of Bosnia and hope that ethnic 'homogenization' will guarantee their control over the conquered areas. The notion of an ethnic blend, a mixed marriage or cohabitation is rejected in the name of archaic ideals and the past. The organization of detention camps, in which tens of thousands of civilians are penned under conditions unacceptable to European consciences, represents the logical outcome of an implacable desire for ethnic hegemony. Serbian determination seems to have paid off judging by the proportions of the gigantic exodus triggered by the campaign of terror. The carving up of a democratically proclaimed republic is currently under completion as Bosnia's Moslems gradually become the Palestinians of the Balkans.

Humanitarian aid as political evasion

The Yugoslav crisis has plunged the humanitarian organizations into deep confusion. The elementary principles of humanity have been systematically trampled on and humanitarian interventions have been found to be well-nigh impossible in the combat zones. The wounded have not been evacuated, hospitals and ambulances have been singled out as prime targets and relief organizations have been cynically manipulated. In spite of the declarations on observance of humanitarian principles signed on 5 November 1991 in the Hague by the presidents of the six republics, in spite of the reiteration of these principles on three further occasions in Geneva by the plenipotentiaries, in spite yet again of local agreements, relief organizations are in most instances unable to carry out their mandate.

Confronted with 'ethnic cleansing', humanitarian organizations face a dilemma: helping to evacuate the population to protect it is tantamount to accepting the 'ethnic cleansing' logic but refusing such aid means abandoning civilians in the hands of the militias. When the main objective of a conflict is to turn populations into refugees, humanitarian aid is reduced to impotence.

As the conflict drags on, independent humanitarian agencies have gradually been pushed to the sidelines, while the European countries turned to relief activism as the only response to the strategy of 'ethnic cleansing' and territorial conquest – thus forgetting that the European institutions were founded on the very refusal of such tactics after World War II. For the whole duration of the Bosnian war European leaders contented themselves with calling for the protection of relief convoys, never taking any initiatives likely to put a stop to bombardments, massacres and deportations. When political responsibility and principles of humanity retreat so radically, humanitarian aid is no longer the conscience – good or bad – of the West, but a mask for shameful abdication.

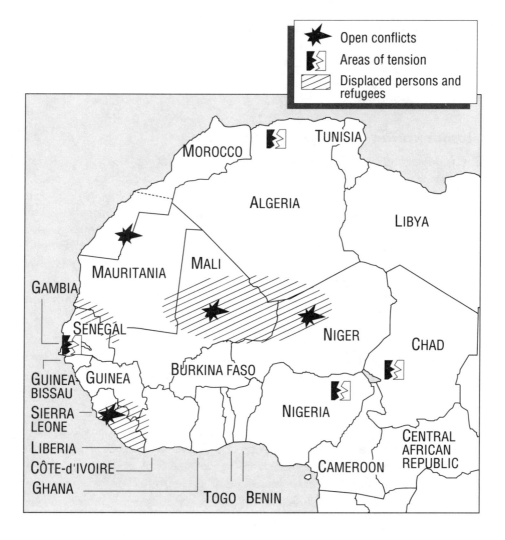

Open conflicts

Areas of tension

Displaced persons and refugees

WEST AFRICA

Introduction

Over the last few years West Africa has entered a period of unrest. These are not exactly wars. No shocking images are reaching us from this part of the world, for the deaths, unless counted over the total period, do not add up to thousands. However, hidden under this false impression of stability, numerous masked conflicts are developing and are likely to go on indefinitively. Displaced populations often despair of ever returning home, for insecurity is still rife there.

Tension in the region is particularly focused on two areas. One of these follows the dividing line between North Africa and sub-Saharan Africa, which runs along the continent from west to east. Along this border almost all the countries are torn apart by a north-south conflict. Another drags on in Liberia where the 1990 war has still not ended. To varying degrees, all the neighbouring countries are involved in this conflict which is a threat to the region as a whole.

From the Atlantic to the Red Sea, the rift – and the clash – between the Berber-Arab and black African cultures has always had dire consequences. For the past few years it has become more and more obvious, particularly in Niger and in Mali where the Tuaregs have rebelled against the central government, which is in the hands of the 'southerners'. In April 1992, after two years of conflict, the rebels in Mali signed a peace agreement with the government under Algerian arbitration. Algeria is concerned as several tens of thousands of Tuaregs have taken refuge on its territory. However, incidents have carried on regardless and the Tuareg people who have sought refuge in the neighbouring countries to escape the massacres of the national army will doubtless take time to return to northern Mali.

In Niger, the situation is even more worrying. The rebellion, which started later, is less clear-cut. The army, over which the transition government has little control, has imposed a de facto martial law in the north.

Further victims of the racial rift are the 100,000 black Mauritanian refugees, in the Senegal river valley in Mali and Senegal, who are still awaiting the opportunity to return to their home country. They were 'deported' following the massacres which occurred in April 1989 between Mauritanians and Senegalese in both countries and have largely been forgotten in spite of the re-establishment of diplomatic relations between Senegal and Mauritania on 23 April 1992.

In Chad, from the start of independence, north-south antagonism led to a recurrent conflict which seems far from being solved. Although tension between the north and the south has been masked for the last few years by internal conclicts between the 'northeners', the rift is deep and could easily reappear. Lastly, the confrontation between the black and Arab cultures continues towards the east in Sudan, where it has turned into a particularly cruel war.

The Liberian abcess

Of the coastal countries, Liberia represents the most dangerous abcess. The offensive undertaken by Charles Taylor and his men in December 1989, interrupted by the intervention of the peacekeeping force of the Community of West African States (ECOWAS), has led to an unbearable status quo for the population. There are now two Liberias: one is in the hands of the transitional government, acting in good faith, but lacking means of action and holding only the capital, Monrovia; the other under the National Patriotic Front of Liberia (NPFL) led by Charles Taylor, who continues to 'reign' over the rest of the country.

The peace agreement signed in October 1991 in Yamoussoukro did not come into effect. The NPFL refuses to lay down its arms as sporadic fighting continues with the former soldiers of the dead dictator, Samuel Doe, based in Sierra Leone. The intervention force, made up mainly of Nigerian, Senegalese and Ghanaian soldiers, has been trapped in the conflict. Deployed late in the war, it has become the target of uncontrolled soldiers.

The population is being taken hostage, refugee camps in Guinea are becoming permanent features, cheap weapons are circulating thoughout the entire area and the cost in human lives is high – the Nigerian troops are thought to have lost 800 men in two years. In time, the Liberian conflict is likely to contaminate the whole of the sub-region – all the more so given the ominous uncertainty that threatens the future of certain neighbouring countries.

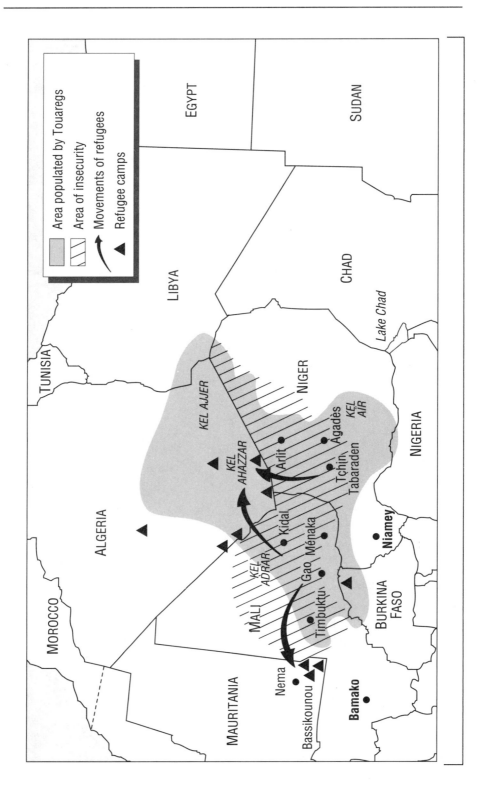

Legend:
- Area populated by Touaregs
- Area of insecurity
- Movements of refugees
- Refugee camps

TUAREGS

Drought, the decline of pastoral nomadism, social exclusion, repression, exodus ... . Today over a million Tuaregs wander between the Sahara and the Sahel and try to survive in a territory shared between five states: Mali, Niger, Algeria, Burkina Faso and Libya.

In Mali and Niger, the Tuaregs have been in rebellion for the past two years and the civilian population has been caught up in a maelstrom of violence and blind reprisals which have cast out into exile over 100,000 people, who have fled mainly to Algeria and Mauritania.

From nomads to minorities

The Tuaregs, of Berber origin, settled in the south Sahara mountains in the seventh century. They were the link between the Moslem Berber-Arab world of North Africa and the great black kingdoms of Mali and Benin, and reigned over a desert territory as large as Western Europe. Making their livelihood out of caravan trading, they controlled trans-Saharan trade by levying tolls on the caravans. The French, who arrived in the region in 1850, had to face armed resistance which lasted for over 60 years. After their surrender in 1917, the Tuaregs continued to reject French domination. Turning in on themselves, they refused to cooperate and did not send their children to school.

When independence came at the beginning of the 1960s, the Sahara was shared between Algeria, Niger, Mali etc. The frontiers hindered free circulation of men and their herds of livestock, reducing their vital room for manoeuvre in periods of drought. The very creation of states turned the Tuaregs into a minority within their traditional territory. A double economic and political time-lag was added to this psychological split. Trans-Saharan trade collapsed and the exchange of basic products such as salt, sugar, dates, tea, semolina, but also livestock, was then submitted to customs duty and other taxes. In the newly created states, the Tuaregs were kept away from central administration. They were to pay for their former status as dominators and their refusal of schooling and modernity. The black population of Mali and Niger saw those who had previously taxed, plundered and employed them as servants or slaves, in a position of inferiority.

In 1963 in Mali, an armed revolt was quashed in bloodshed and this led to a large-scale exodus towards the neighbouring countries. A new form of interior resistance and passive isolation started. The north was placed under military administration. In Libya at the end of the 1960s their forced sedentarization remained largely unnoticed. In Algeria they were assimilated by force and now carry only derisory political, economic and demographic weight. In Burkina Faso, they represent a small minority of pastoral farmers and are relatively well integrated. In Niger, as in Mali, the north of the country, where the Tuaregs live, is excluded from most development projects. Uranium, which ensured a major part of the economic balance of Niger, is in Tuareg country, but little of the resources generated by uranium mining are used to develop the north of the country.

The successive droughts of 1973–74 and 1984–85 accentuated the process of exclusion and impoverishment. The desert gained ground, men and animals died by thousands while international aid was misappropriated by the ruling government. The survivors tried to go back to the pastures in the south, but encountered hostility from the sedentary farmers of Niger and Mali, who were themselves severely affected by the drought. Several thousand Tuaregs sought refuge in the south of Algeria where, without their livestock, without resources, they became 'assisted'. A new cast of Tuaregs was born, the 'ishoumars', which is a phonetic rendering of 'chômeurs', the French for unemployed. Others left for Libya, where the younger ones were obliged to do their military service and were sometimes sent off by force to fight in Lebanon or Chad.

In 1986, Algeria officially decided to expel the 20,000 to 30,000 Tuaregs from Mali and Niger who had settled in the country. Algeria thus expressed its reticence to give shelter in its troubled south to this 'fluctuating' population that its Libyan neighbour was prompt to manipulate and whose movements hindered border control. In 1989 the governments of Niger and Mali offered to allow the refugees to go back to their countries with promises of reintegration incentives. Those who took the risk of doing so were parked in camps and never received the aid promised.

The time of revolt

In Niger, in May 1990, some young Tuaregs attacked the prison of Tchin Tabaraden. The army, powerless to catch the culprits, took reprisals on the civilian population,

The ravages of measles in the refugee camps

Since their arrival in Mauritania, the 30,000 Tuaregs and Malian Moors in the refugee camps have survived in very bad conditions of health and hygiene. In May 1992, an epidemiological investigation revealed a very high mortality rate: four deaths per 10,000 people per day, that is double of what is usually judged to be acceptable in an emergency situation. As usual, children were the first victims: a quarter of all children under the age of five had died in one year.

Nearly half these deaths were due to an epidemic of measles which broke out during the first months of 1992. Among the 2,000 families gathered together in the Bassikounou camp, over 600 people died of this disease. The sedentary population, which had either already been vaccinated against measles or in contact with it, was not too badly affected by the epidemic. However, many non-immunized nomadic families were decimated.

The epidemic spread very fast since these people were grouped together. The effects of measles were aggravated by the state of health of these refugees, who were already suffering from malnutrition and weakened from their long wanderings. Measles is above all dangerous because of its complications: lung infections, acute diarrhoea and malnutrition. On weakened bodies and with inadequate medical environment, these complications are more frequent than in developed countries.

This epidemic once again illustrates the severity of measles in Africa. It is an absolute priority to vaccinate all children against measles in refugee or displaced persons' camps, just as they must be supplied with food and water. Although effective vaccines are available, the vaccination campaign must extend its coverage up to 95 per cent of the target population to effectively prevent and control these epidemics, since large groups of people are a fertile ground for the transmission of viruses.

massacring nearly 200 people. The trauma of this massacre was felt in the whole of the Tuareg territory. It became a ferment which gave birth to more radical militant movements for the institution of 'integral federalism' in Niger. In mid 1992 the situation in the north was still extremely tense.

A month later revolt started in Mali with the attack on the prison in Menaka. For several months the rebels occupied the north of the country and held off the army which in turn retaliated against the population and livestock. The Tuaregs demanded recognition of their identity and autonomous government of the northern regions. A first peace agreement signed at Tamanrasset in January 1991 between the Malian Tuaregs and the military government of Moussa Traoré was not respected, leading to division among the Tuareg fighters, resumption of guerrilla warfare and sometimes banditry.

From April 1991 onwards, severe reprisals against the civilian population were taken by the army which, given a place of lesser importance by the transition government, had become difficult to control. The northern regions lived in a climate of perpetual insecurity due to the exactions of the soldiers and looting by uncontrolled Tuareg factions. The black population organized self-defence committees supported by the army. Skirmishes came to look more and more like racial violence. Then a large-scale exodus of Malian Tuaregs started towards Algeria, Niger and above all towards Mauritania. A climate of terror arose between the communities with long-lasting consequences that will be difficult to forget. In two years the conflict has caused over 3000 deaths and produced more than 100,000 refugees.

After difficult negotiations, a new peace agreement was reached in April 1992: the national Pact, signed by the Tuareg movement and the new democratically elected Malian government, gave the northern regions a different status within Malian unity. If it is respected, this pact could set an example for the resolution of the conflict in Niger and open the way for the return of refugees.

The distress of the refugees

In Mauritania, the 30,000 Tuareg and Moorish refugees from Mali are mainly gathered together in three camps in the extreme south-east of the country where they receive medical assistance and food aid from relief agencies. Most of them arrived completely destitute with nothing but a few cooking ustensils, sometimes a few head of livestock. Assistance for these refugees is difficult to organize over 1500 km away from the Mauritanian capital in a desert region where the local population is itself struggling to survive. After over a year of exile, the major problems linked to lack of water and insufficient food rations are not yet entirely solved. Epidemics of measles have caused numerous deaths among both children and adults weakened by hunger and exhaustion due to their long journey into exile.

In Burkina Faso, about 15,000 Malian Tuareg refugees are being helped by the Burkinabe government, the United Nations High Commissioner for Refugees and the local Tuaregs. In Algeria the refugees – 50,000 Malian Tuaregs, 15,000 Tuaregs from Niger – are in great need of food and medical care. They are mainly helped by Algerian Kabyles and Tuaregs, who give them the means to survive.

Nowadays, the Tuareg population, in Mali, in Niger and in the countries they have fled to, live in great precariousness and constant fear: fear as to their political future and their place in states where they have become minorities, fear for their future in regions that suffer from great economic instability, fear, also, for their safety in regions that international aid finds hard to reach. Prevailing insecurity in the north of Mali and Niger, the closing of certain zones by the army and looters' attacks on vehicles are all obstacles to humanitarian aid. Relief agencies have had to reduce their presence, increasing yet again the isolation of the civilian population.

Drought areas
Drought centre
Principal famine areas

Southern Africa

Introduction

For many farmers in southern Africa, the 1992 drought is likely to be the worst they have ever suffered, although in the past they have already seen their crops wither in the burning sun and their livestock die off for lack of grazing. In 1992 the grain production of Southern Africa only reached half its usual level and countries in this region are having to buy grain on the international market or call for food aid to compensate their deficit.

A large part of their immediate needs can be met by traditional commercial agreements and the so-called 'planned' relief programme upon which millions of Mozambicans have been relying for years. However, the fast launch of emergency food relief is likely to be more problematic because of hold-ups in funding agreements and logistic bottlenecks. Ten million tonnes will have to transit through the ports in this region and be sent into the threatened areas. The estimated population affected by drought in the entire region, except for South Africa, was 17 million for 1992, according to the United Nations. Although these distressing figures tend to substantiate the idea of a whole region threatened with famine, the reality is actually more complex: the drought is causing a combination of severe economic and social problems but only the areas affected by widespread insecurity are really at risk of famine.

The drought strikes at the worst possible moment for a region only just emerging from years of war and in the throes of tackling the difficult process of opening up the political spectrum. In Zambia, where the effects of drought have combined with the impact of economic decline, the new democratically elected government, just about to come to grips with painful reforms, has been caught off balance. In Zimbabwe, tensions are likely to rise between the government, discredited by its management of the crisis, and the threatened populations – especially those of the Eastern Highlands and Masvingo regions, who have already suffered localized famine in the recent past. In Malawi, drought is striking at a crucial moment for the decaying dictatorship. In South Africa it throws into sharp relief the difference in treatment between blacks and whites, but at the same time it has allowed emergency units to appear that cover the whole ethnic and political spectrum. These are real laboratories for putting integration into practice.

Of course the drought is due to unfavourable climatic factors, rainfall between December 1991 and March 1992 having been insufficient. However, a few large areas have been spared: Angola, northern Malawi and northern Mozambique, Swaziland and the west of Zambia. But drought does not explain everything. Previously observed famine situations have been closely linked to government incapacity to prevent the effects of drought. There are very few countries – Botswana and Namibia for instance – who have in fact set up a warning system and taken heed of it since the beginning of 1992. Zimbabwe also has an alarm system, but a large part of its grain reserves was recently sold to make up for a shortage of foreign currency as the countryside was beginning to feel the pinch of drought.

This drought and the famine which affect the rural population in some areas of scarcity or chronic insecurity – the Zimbabwean Lowveld, eastern Zambia, southern Mozambique – reveal the social fragility of these countries. Drought is a source of agricultural bankruptcy, dwindling mining activity, unemployment, inflation and collapse of foreign currency reserves. Refugees are likely to be the first hit by these economic difficulties. Their situation, already dramatic in many countries, is likely to become even more precarious. Mozambican refugees are all the more vulnerable because they vie with local populations for international relief, particularly in Malawi. On the farms in Zimbabwe, Mozambicans are first in line for dismissal. They are also the first to be made redundant on farms and in the mines in South Africa.

Nevertheless, very few Mozambicans consider going home with equanimity: on the contrary, many want to flee a country devastated by war and struck this year by famine. The current drought in southern Africa is, in fact, having tragic consequences in the centre and south of Mozambique. In the provinces of Gaza, Inhambane, Manica and Sofala, the general climate of insecurity hinders deliveries of regular relief supplies and the population is more than ever trapped in the vice of war and famine.

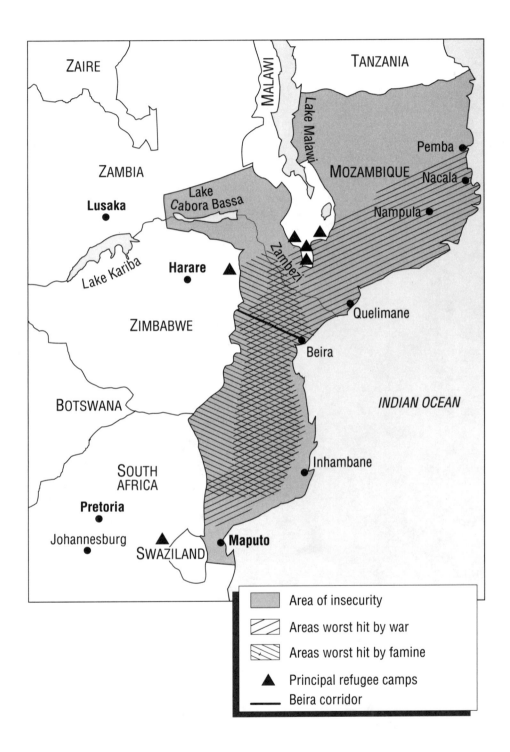

ZAIRE

ZAMBIA

Lusaka

Lake Kariba

Harare

ZIMBABWE

BOTSWANA

SOUTH
AFRICA

Pretoria

Johannesburg

SWAZILAND

MALAWI

Lake Malawi

Lake
Cabora Bassa

Zambezi

TANZANIA

MOZAMBIQUE

Pemba

Nacala

Nampula

Quelimane

Beira

INDIAN OCEAN

Inhambane

Maputo

☐	Area of insecurity
▨	Areas worst hit by war
▨	Areas worst hit by famine
▲	Principal refugee camps
—	Beira corridor

Mozambique

We are constantly being reminded of the situation in Mozambique, with about a hundred international relief agencies already providing assistance and calls for aid coming in regularly. Over the last few years it has become no more than a desperate column of ever worsening statistics: around a million dead since the beginning of the conflict, close to two million refugees in neighbouring countries, over three million displaced persons inside the country, the highest child mortality rate in the world (one third of its children under the age of five die), estimated requirements in food aid reaching a million tonnes of grain for 1992, a quarter of the population (i.e. over four million people) chronically dependent on international aid and, this year, three million people threatened with famine … . These grim figures and the monotony of calls for aid cannot hide the despair of a population trapped for 20 years by war and now struck by famine, which is due less to climatic hazards than to human error and misdeeds.

Fifteen years of terror

The dramatic aspect of the situation in Mozabique is that the current drought – which at any other time would have been controllable – is today developing into famine. The agricultural surplus in the north which ought to compensate for the deficits recorded in the centre and south of the country, cannot in fact be transported in sufficient quantities into the areas at risk. This state of affairs is mainly linked to war, insecurity and a falling apart of the post-colonial state, which owes nothing to chance.

In 1975, at the end of Portuguese administration, Frelimo, which had succeeded in taking military control of several provinces in the north and the west, took over a country which was closely interwoven into the South African economy, and on a wider scale into southern African geopolitics: each year hundreds of thousands of workers went to work in the goldmines in Transvaal. The port of Lourenço Marques, which was to become Maputo, was the natural outlet for exportations from the South African Vaal, while access to the ports of Beira and Nampula was vital for Ian Smith's Rhodesia which was later to become Zimbabwe. Mozambique's interdependence with its neighbours was obvious: its economy was based on services, its roads and ports ensured 90 per cent of its income, while salaries from South African expatriates funded public revenue. Interdependence meant political solidarity too: Samora Machel's Frelimo, which had led the fight for independence against Portugal, was keen to support the ANC's struggle in South Africa, host supply bases for Robert Mugabe's troops fighting in Rhodesia, and to build a socialist state to free southern Africa from its dependence on the South African economy.

Mozambique is still paying for this daring challenge. In 1977 Ian Smith's Rhodesia encouraged the creation of a rebel movement, Renamo, the National Resistance Movement for Mozambique. It is a dangerous cocktail of farmers hostile to collectivization of land, deserters from cooperatives and state farms and former members of the colonial army. They were given financial support by former Portuguese settlers and were backed up by South Africa's logistics and secret service. This dangerous association, as some of its founders now confess, gave birth to a monster which became uncontrollable. Over the years, the rebellion nested in the countryside, taking advantage of the rural population's opposition to government projects to group the peasants into collective structures. Little by little, Renamo became encapsulated into rural society, its only aim being its own reproduction in warfare and the destruction of the symbols of a socialist state that the guerrillas, who had by now become apparatchiks, wanted to build. Primary schools, rural health centres, agricultural cooperatives and state farms were their main targets and the asphalt roads, vital arteries for access to the ports, became unusable in most of the country.

Renamo's methods are simple and brutal: the rebels swoop down on villages, burn official buildings, terrorize the villagers and take away their harvests. Everything is permitted. Hands and ears are cut off, people are beheaded as an example to others, children are abducted who will later become rebel soldiers. They kill, they steal and they mine the outskirts of the villages. This terrorist policy has killed hundreds of thousands over the past 15 years. In the least serious cases, the local Renamo lords requisition villagers or abduct townsfolk to use as porters or servants.

Incapable of quashing the rebellion, exasperated by their own ineffectiveness, bewildered by the contradictions of a government which has abandoned socialism for IMF-inspired reforms, the government soldiers, poorly paid and badly fed, are just as bad as the rebels as far as exactions and lack of discipline are concerned. When the rebels

Refugees in Malawi

Malawi sticks out like a wedge into the territory of Mozambique which is ravaged by civil war. Since 1986, the intensification of military operations in the Mozambican province of Zambezia has led to an ever-increasing flow of refugees, fleeing war and starvation. Malawi, with hardly nine million inhabitants, today shelters over a million Mozambicans in its camps.

Through concerted action between the international relief agencies and the Malawian Ministry of Health, the refugees' situation is relatively satisfactory, perhaps even better than that of the Malawian population itself, as the death rate, the level of nutrition and the vaccination campaigns show. However, it remains precarious: the two main preoccupations are epidemics (cholera, which is endemic in Malawi, ravaged the overpopulated camps in 1990–91) and the food supply, which is totally dependent on international aid. Eighteen thousand cases of pellagra, a sometimes fatal deficiency disease, occurred in the camps in 1990 because of an interruption in the distribution of peanuts, which are rich in niacin. This shows how unstable the nutritional situation is and how vulnerable the refugees are to the least variation in their food ration.

Malawi is currently faced with an uncertain political future and with the effects of the drought in the south of the country, where three-quarters of the refugees are grouped. In the months to come, the needs for food aid for both communities will be enormous and difficult to meet in an enclaved country. If the Malawian population itself is not well provided for, it will be even more difficult to transport food to the camps. An 'end of reign' atmosphere after 28 years of exclusive dictatorship, combined with the population's weariness of the refugees, does not contribute to a spirit of conciliation. In Malawi, as elsewhere, the international community has an essential role to play to ensure assistance and protection is given to the refugees.

attack convoys of food aid, the soldiers responsible for their protection help themselves liberally and do not disdain looting and fleecing the peasants.

Thus conflict continues in the countryside although its very origins are almost forgotten. The Cold War is over, South Africa confirms that it has given up supporting Renamo, Frelimo is on good terms with the Western world, the government army is trained by British military instructors, but the war, which has escaped all governmental control, is little by little being privatized and goes on regardless. It henceforth has its own logic and continues to ruin the lives of millions of civilians while international opinion remains silent and indifferent.

Mozambicans in South Africa

South Africa and Mozambique share a 500-km borderline which provides a sharp contrast between a – partially – very prosperous country and a ghost land with a rural poulation living in a permanent state of fear. Of the 400,000 Mozambicans who have succeeded in crossing the border since the beginning of the exodus in 1985:

■ Less than a quarter have a work contract in a mine or on a farm. According to a practice going back to the 19th century, the Mozambican government recruits them for South Africa, always in search of docile manpower.

■ Over half of them stay illegally on white South African territory and become familiar with illicit South Africa, sometimes even with slavery, and frequently forced repatriation to Mozambique (50,000 people in 1991).

■ Lastly, over 100,000 have been able to find temporary refuge in the Gazankulu and Kangwane 'homelands'. The South African authorities tolerate this as long as refugees are kept within the borders of the 'homelands'.

This tolerance is quite likely to end with the dismantling of the 'homelands' in view, and also because of the consensus between the government and the ANC on the necessity of giving priority to national problems. The urban population, regardless of their ethnic background, agrees on the rejection of the Mozambicans, held responsible for all the problems in the country: violence, unemployment. Ironic as it may seem, the Mozambican refugees are likely to bear the brunt of the bumpy departure of apartheid, when opening up the 'homelands' may lead to closing the national borders.

What becomes of the refugees in South Africa will depend mostly on the ability of the United Nations High Commissioner for Refugees to convince the government to leave it the full power of its mandate and to resist any premature repatriation of refugees to a country where rumours of a ceasefire do not necessarily amount to a lull in the field, far from it.

The archipelago of fear and hunger

Mozambique is today the archipelago of fear and hunger. In the countryside, the government army forcibly gathers the villagers together in 'protected villages' or groups them around the towns, as the Portuguese colonizers did. Within these controlled areas the peasants are no longer likely to come into contact with the Renamo rebels, to give them their harvests, or to supply them with young soldiers. However, these groups of people are now far away from their villages, they can no longer cultivate their land

and are totally dependent on international aid. The depopulation of the countryside aggravates the effects of the drought: the land is only sporadically cultivated, roads are often cut and the isolation of the provinces makes trade between hitherto complementary regions difficult.

Thus a new geographical layout is appearing, made up of isolated towns, surrounded by a narrow security perimeter, and of hazardous and practically inaccessible countryside. Nobody really knows what has become of the civilian population in the uncontrolled areas where Renamo is at large. In some regions the peasants are dying in silence, trapped by drought and insecurity, out of reach of international relief. Elsewhere they end up on the outskirts of towns in the hope of finding help. Pushed by hunger and fear, the peasants of Mozambique have set out to look for a little peace and some help. According to the United Nations over three million Mozambicans were displaced persons in 1992. Some camp outside the towns, others, dressed in tree-bark and fed on roots, wander across the countryside in a pitiful state, while two million people are refugees in neighbouring countries, half of them in Malawi, totally dependent on international aid.

International attention, somewhat tired of the recurrent nature of the crisis and frequent calls for help, has been indirectly attracted back to Mozambique by the drought which is currently affecting all the countries of southern Africa. But apart from the logistical difficulties of handling the emergency, aid itself leads to political problems. On the one hand, if it is distributed in urban areas where the displaced persons are packed, it will accentuate the rural exodus and reinforce Frelimo's authority. On the other hand, in order to have access to the countryside or guarantee the safety of food aid convoys, the United Nations has to negotiate with Renamo, which is liable to boost the rebels' international legitimacy.

Thus the United Nations was able to obtain from both parties the opening of 'humanitarian corridors' to allow food aid to be sent inside the country. But, as peace talks are indefinitely resumed or broken off, truces are invariably broken and agreements rarely come into effect on the spot, the war in Mozambique does not seem to be anywhere near to ending. Faced with the diversity of local situations, relief organizations must remain vigilant and intervene in time to bring help to populations at risk. The crucial problem in Mozambique today in the field of emergency aid is that of access to victims. Faced with this interminable conflict, the international community has an essential role to play to preserve and widen the space for relief action. Otherwise the civilian population will be further trapped between war and starvation.

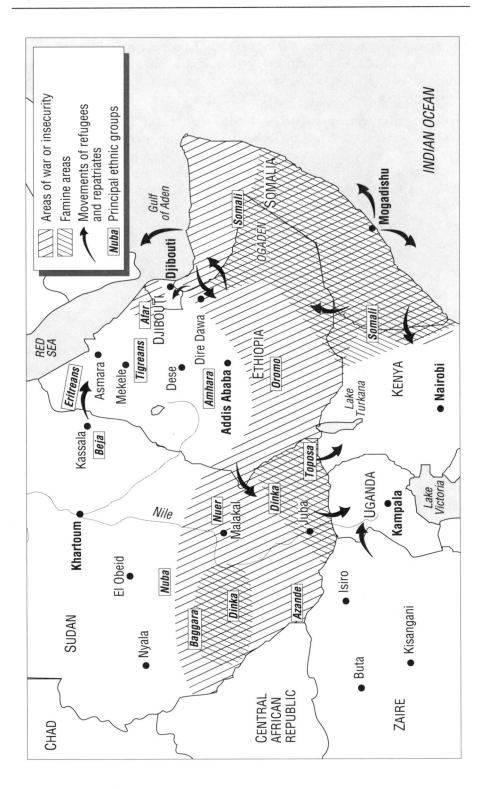

The horn of africa

Introduction

If one needed an example of great human distress spanning more than 10 years, one would choose the Horn of Africa. It has the doubtful privilege of having one of the world's longest records for war, drought and forced movements of population.

During the last 10 years, the Horn of Africa has sheltered nearly half of all the refugees in Africa. The first reason for this has been the length and violence of the conflicts. Secondly, its fragile ecosystem has simply been ruined by the most absurd agricultural policy and lasting instability. The number of Eritrean refugees in Sudan rose from 30,000 in 1967 to over 350,000 in 1984–85. For 1984–85 again, Sudan alone came top of the list of host countries with nearly 200,000 refugees from Chad, fleeing drought and civil war, over 300,000 Ethiopians, mainly from Tigré, trying to escape repression by Mengistu's regime, 210,000 Ugandans … . As for Somalia, it paid a high price for its defeat in the 1978 war with Ethiopia: it first sheltered the Somalis from Ogaden threatened with attack by Ethiopian troops, before it became the refuge of Ethiopian farmers affected by collectivization.

Lastly, at the end of the 1980s, nearly 400,000 Sudanese fled to Ethiopia from war in the south of their country. These human flows were so gigantic that they became a key element in the strategies of both governments and armed movements. Not only do refugees confer a specific political legitimacy, as recipients of international aid they also provide financial support. And through forced recruitment, they unwillingly provide 'human resources' to governments and guerrilla movements.

The 1984–85 drought enabled international opinion to grasp the complex relationship between forced movements of populations, war and famine. The map of starvation did in fact largely correspond to that of regions affected by war, mass displacements of population clearly resulting from the combined effects of drought and insecurity. Each of the warring parties was trying to take advantage of the situation: the Ethiopian regime tried to justify its policy of forced displacement of populations from the north to the south and west of the country, and in Somalia, the refugees of the Ogaden war were often turned into back-up troops for Siad Barre's regime.

The region's political landscape changed radically in a short period of time: an Islamic junta came to power in Khartoum in June 1989, Siad Barre was overthrown in January 1991, Mengistu in May 1991 and the Djibouti crisis happened six months later. In Sudan, the new regime hindered any intervention by relief agencies while more intensive fighting spilled over the borders of southern Sudan into Kordofan and Darfour, increasing the number of displaced persons. The Somali situation was no less dramatic: the collapse of all state administration caused the unrest to engulf the whole country, whether in the form of clan fighting, conflicts between political and military factions or, to put it more crudely, mere social banditry. This situation of extreme insecurity has led to large-scale famine and a mass exodus of refugees to Kenya, Ethiopia, Djibouti and even Yemen.

In Ethiopia, the coming to power of the guerrillas in an exhausted country, and the support that they received from the United States, gave rise to hopes of stability, for a time at least. But the social problems – particularly linked to the rapid demobilization of over 300,000 soldiers of Mengistu's former army, left without any resources – and the political problems brought about by the newly-introduced 'ethnic federalism' rapidly triggered off unrest in several parts of the country. The rivalry between the Oromos – who make up nearly 40 per cent of the country's population – and the central government meant increasing insecurity in the south, especially as Ogaden was feeling the repercussions of the Somalian war.

The drought which has struck the Afars and Somalis adds further to the tension between the peripheral regions and the central government. Ethiopia also has to cope with the return of former refugees – there were 500,000 in 1990–91 alone – most of them from camps in Somalia. Another 500,000 refugees, mainly of Somali origin, are living in Ethiopia today, not to mention the hundreds of thousands of displaced Ethiopians within the country, also in great need of help. In a region racked by profound destitution, the future of Ethiopia seems more than ever jeopardized by the contagious effects of Somali anarchy and the Sudanese tragedy.

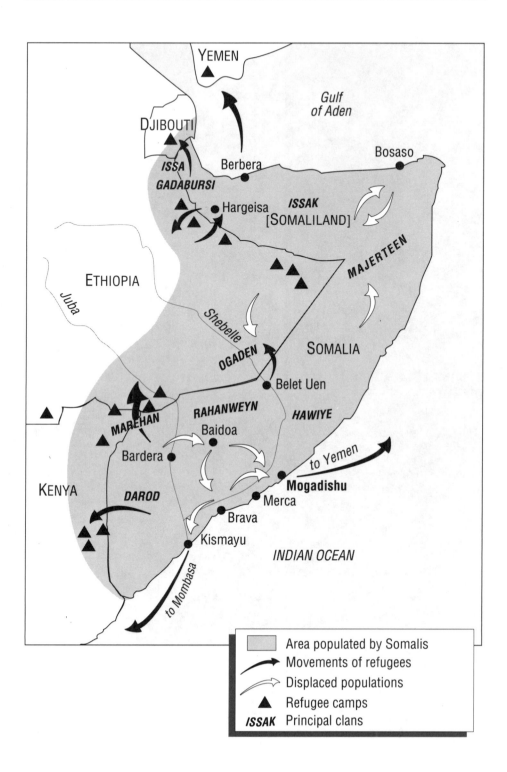

YEMEN

Gulf of Aden

DJIBOUTI

Bosaso

Berbera

ISSA
GADABURSI

Hargeisa

ISSAK
[SOMALILAND]

MAJERTEEN

ETHIOPIA

Juba

Shebelle

OGADEN

SOMALIA

Belet Uen

RAHANWEYN

HAWIYE

Baidoa

MARÉHAN

Bardera

to Yemen

Mogadishu

KENYA

DAROD

Merca

Brava

Kismayu

INDIAN OCEAN

to Mombasa

	Area populated by Somalis
	Movements of refugees
	Displaced populations
▲	Refugee camps
ISSAK	Principal clans

SOMALIA

A 'country adrift', 'Mogadishu, city of starvation', 'Mayhem in Somalia' ... so many clichés try to sum up an unprecedented tragedy. Never was a country drawn into such a maelstrom of violence on the brink of collective suicide. In this arrowhead-shaped country, jutting out into the Indian Ocean, no region has been spared by the war. Repeated fighting and massacres, looting, systematic destruction and the flight all over the country of terrorized people have little by little transformed the shortages into scarcity, and scarcity into famine. Out of an estimated total of seven million Somalis, four million need emergency food aid and half of these are currently dying of starvation.

Four years of terror

Before his fall, on 27 January 1991, General Mohamed Siad Barre had already greatly contributed to the destruction of Somalia by exacerbating the rifts between clans and using savage repression to maintain his iron-fisted rule.

In May 1988, the rebels of the Somali National Movement (SNM), who rightly accused the government of neglecting the north and persecuting its inhabitants, the Isaaq, briefly held the towns of Hargeisa and Burao. In reaction to this hasty offensive, the government's retaliation took the form of an extermination campaign: both towns were bombarded and partly destroyed and Hargeisa was mined to prevent its inhabitants from going back. Tens of thousands of civilians were killed, and over 500,000 people fled to Ethiopia.

The Isaaq rebellion spread. In 1989 desertion was on the increase: the Ogaden clan, then the Hawiye, broke away from the decaying regime. Siad Barre tried to compromise, but it was already too late – he no longer ruled the Mogadishu region.

The Hawiye, who originally came from the centre and were well implanted in Mogadishu, found themselves on the front line. They witnessed the progressive foundering of the capital, paralysed by power cuts, crushed by repression and crammed to bursting point with thousands of peasants fleeing violence in the country.

An insurrection broke out in Mogadishu at the end of 1990. Driven to the brink of defeat, Siad Barre resisted for two weeks, using heavy artillery on the 'bandits'; murdering hundreds of civilians. At last he retreated towards the south, abandoning the drained capital to looters and indiscriminate shooting.

From then on, clan conflicts became the prime element of local politics. The interim president, Ali Mahdi Mohamed was rejected by the other clans. In May 1991, the Isaaq proclaimed the independence of the Republic of Somaliland in the north of the country while the members of Siad Barre's clan, the Marehan, grouped together and took up arms in the south. Attacks and counter-attacks followed, sometimes just outside the capital. Ali Mahdi's power is even questioned within his own clan by General Mohamed Farah 'Aideed'. In November 1991, Mogadishu flared up in a merciless combat opposing the two Hawiye sub-clans. All semblance of law disappeared in the capital, transformed into a closed battlefield where the clans fought for the remains of a state which had long since collapsed.

When the fighting died down on 3 March 1992, Mogadishu was no more than a heap of ruins cut in two by a virtual front line. In four months the fighting had killed or injured nearly 25,000 and caused thousands of people to flee. The survivors were crammed into crumbling houses, without water, electricity, wood for heating or even food.

The situation was no better in the rest of the country. In the bush the wells were contaminated, the livestock partly disperserd or easy prey for looters. In the fertile area between the Juba and Shebelle rivers all seeds had been stolen, the farmers driven away and the tractors turned into war machines. Uprooted populations were wandering around the whole country to flee the fighting or were seeking refuge in neighbouring countries to try to find safety and the means to survive. Thousands of boat people swarmed aboard makeshift boats and cargo ships to try and reach Yemen or the port of Mombasa, Kenya. Refugees fled en masse to Kenya and Ethiopia and hundreds of thousands of displaced persons were thrown on to the roads by the fighting that flared up thoughout the country.

Merca, Brava, Baidoba, were crying out with famine as early as spring 1992. The situation was particularly dramatic in Merca where thousands of displaced persons had drifted: the mortality rate, which was estimated at 20 per thousand per year in Somalia before the war, reached 163 per thousand in April 1992 among the displaced persons in the region and 241 per thousand for under-fives. This meant that in one year, one child out of four died, mainly from lack of food. Malnutrition rates were

The refugees in north-eastern Kenya

The continuing deterioration of the situation in Somalia has led to a mass exodus into Kenya, which started in 1988. However this remained relatively limited until the fall of Siad Barre, when the fighting spread to engulf all the south of the country, forcing an ever-increasing number of people to flee. At the beginning of 1992, this exodus took on dramatic proportions, further amplified by famine. In July 1992, over a thousand people crossed the border each day and the number of Somali refugees, over 90,000 in January, reached 230,000, not to mention the tens of thousands of Somalis who entered Kenya through unofficial channels.

In early 1992, the overwhelmed Kenyan authorities called on international relief organizations to take charge of the overpopulated camps where hygiene and food conditions were rapidly degenerating. The situation appeared all the more critical since the north of Kenya, where the refugee camps are located, was itself struck by severe drought. This drought turned into famine because of the government's indifference towards these remote regions and its inability to help the threatened populations in time. As a result, the Somali nomads living in this semi-arid region rapidly found themselves on the verge of famine, turning them into displaced persons wandering about in search of food.

The current relief operations in northern Kenya are made difficult by rampant insecurity: the refugee camps and their poor resources are tempting prey for bandits and armed groups from Somalia. The situation is even more precarious because besides the Somali refugees and the displaced Kenyans, tens of thousands of Sudanese and Ethiopians keep entering Kenya, fleeing the war, famine and insecurity ravaging their country.

just as frightening: for the same period, 90 per cent of the children living in displaced people's camps suffered from malnutrition, 75 per cent of cases were rated severe. The situation in Merca is a tragic illustration of the great distress in Somalia: all the assessments which have since been carried out in newly-accessible regions have consistently shown similar rates of malnutrition. Brought to such a level, these grim statistics no longer make sense, for an entire country is dying from unprecedented famine.

Feeding the hungry without feeding the war

Civil war has partly or totally cut Somalia's four main lifelines: agriculture in the centre, grazing in the north and south, maritime and overland trading and foreign aid – particularly the aid to Ethiopian refugees, which under Barre's regime was one of the

Ethiopian camps: no longer a safe haven

Life becomes more precarious every day in the camps set up on the eastern and southern borders of Ethiopia, where some 500,000 Somalis have taken refuge. On top of general insecurity in the whole of Ethiopia, the effects of the Somali conflict can be felt well into Ogaden and a three-year-long drought has killed off all the livestock, condemning the nomads to starvation.

The general climate of insecurity disrupts the repatriation operations and triggers large-scale population movements. In February 1992, the UNHCR had to shelve its plan to repatriate 300,000 refugees who arrived during the 1988 Hargeisa repression, because of increased fighting in the north of Somalia. In addition, the relief programmes intended for the Ethiopian refugees repatriated from Somalia were disrupted by the mass arrival of new Somali refugees fleeing war and famine, and by the severe consequences of drought that has struck the Somali population of Ethiopia.

Even worse, the relief agencies seeking to bring aid to the threatened populations come up against enormous difficulties. Like Somalia, the south of Ethiopia is awash with arms and riddled with mines. The inhabitants have become easy prey for bandits, uncontrolled groups and soldiers, who levy their lost salaries through killing and looting. In refugee camps, which are totally dependent on international aid, delays in food distribution provoke violent skirmishes and more and more frequently convoys and members of relief agencies are ambushed by looters.

Ethiopia is no longer a haven for the Somalis fleeing tragedy in their country, nor even for its own nomad children or the repatriated refugees. The tragedy is that the conflicts that are tearing apart the Horn of Africa are far from dying down and populations under threat have nowhere left to go.

country's main sources of income. Over the months fighting has destroyed the last resources of Somalia, leaving in its wake a war-torn nation, a dismantled society and uprooted populations in the grip of the most terrible famine.

This ongoing tragedy met with total indifference from the international community for a long time, and the United Nations was conspicuous by its absence. During the whole of 1991, only the ICRC and a handful of humanitarian organizations bore witness to the Somali disaster. For months they attempted both to awaken public opinion and to bring a little humanity to this abandoned country subject only to the law of arms. In conditions of extreme insecurity, they have tried to bring help and protection to the civilian population without, however, being able to curb the fall into disaster. The needs are in fact so enormous that they far exceed the capabilities of non-governmental organizations.

In nutritional aid alone, the distribution of 70,000 tonnes of food a month would be needed. Only a vast emergency relief operation, organized by the United Nations with the political and financial support of Western countries, could adequately meet the requirements of such a disaster. Since December 1991, the UN, impelled by Mr Boutros-Ghali, has tried to regain its footing in the Somali mayhem, but this political will has proved difficult to put into effect on the spot. It is true that Somalia is a real challenge for the UN, obliged to function without any state representative, outside the usual administrative procedures and prior political negotiations, for the sole purpose of feeding the starving.

Aid in Somalia is a vital resource for people threatened with starvation. But food, which is cruelly lacking all over the country, is above all a prize disputed by the warring parties. The fighters themselves have no food and pay themselves by looting. Food is stolen in the ports, hijacked from relief convoys, attacked by anonymous gangs. At this stage, the lack of food is one of the key driving forces of violence. To avoid refuelling it the relief agencies must remain neutral and inventive and ensure distribution on all sides, using all possible channels to reach the starving. And if they aim to break this spiral of violence, they must bring sufficient quantities of grain into the country to reduce tension, lower prices, 'saturate' the warriors, to be able, at last, to help the most vulnerable.

Having fought so long to protect and widen the scope for humanitarian action among the fighters and looters, the relief agencies know only too well how difficult it is to help Somalia; they also know that this difficulty can in no case be a pretext to abstain. Somalia is on the brink of the abyss. Only the UN's involvement and the support of the Western countries will avoid it being finally engulfed by war and famine.

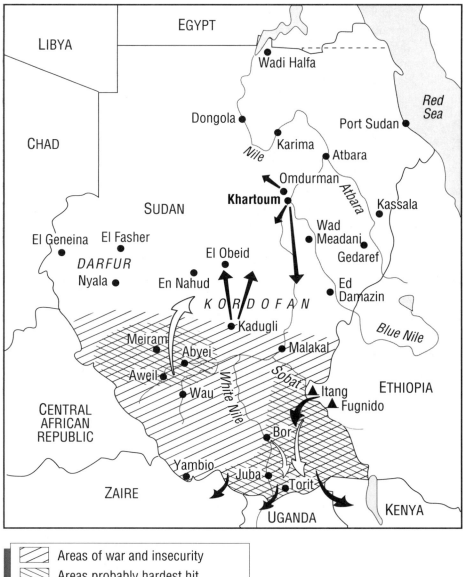

Areas of war and insecurity

Areas probably hardest hit by famine

Displacements of population

Movements of refugees

Deportations of population

Sudan

Among all the acute situations of strife in the world, none is more terrible than the current conflict in Sudan. Firstly because the war that is ravaging the south of the country has become smothered by a curtain of silence: the faint echoes which reach us have become almost inaudible, nevertheless all evoke massacres, famine and forced displacement of population. Secondly because the conflict which is often described as being religious is in fact of a racial nature. Rooted in the rift between the 'Arabs', or rather the black Arab-speaking people, and the black Africans, who are looked down upon – they are still commonly referred to by the name 'abid' which means 'slaves' – this interminable war has been waged in such blatant violation of ordinary rules of humanity that it raises the question of genocide. At the very least, a set of policies of state terrorism almost add up to genocide in their effects. Since 1983, when the conflict began, over 600,000 people have died out of a population assessed in 1983 at 6.3 million. This terrifying depopulation is very likely to continue in 1993. The indifference of the international community to the tragedy can only encourage the 'final solution' to the Sudanese problem.

From war to deportation

The war in southern Sudan is a result of the deep ethnic, religious and historic rift which divides the country. Just before independence in 1955 the first conflict broke out between the black African south, mostly Christian or Animist, and the ruling Arab-Moslem north, which showed little regard for power sharing. The conflict, which lasted 17 years and claimed nearly 200,000 lives, ended in February 1972 with the signature of the Addis Ababa agreement. But the lull was a short one. Fighting resumed in May 1983 when the black troops of the national army, stationed in the south, rose up and

51

created the Sudanese People's Liberation Army (SPLA) in Ethiopia, where they had taken refuge, demanding a change of government in Khartoum and a fair share of resources for all the regions in the country.

The first stage of the conflict (1983–86) could be described as *regular war* if such a term is conceivable. During this period the population was not systematically or deliberately attacked. However, violent fighting caused people to flee in large numbers. Embarrassingly for their SPLA 'liberators', these refugees retreated back into the government garrison towns of the south (particularly Wau, Malakal and Juba) seemingly fleeing from the SPLA. The situation was further complicated in the capital where refugees from the south were joined by 'Arabs' from the north, fleeing the great drought of 1983–84. In 1985, when Marshal Nimeiry's regime was overthrown by a popular uprising, over 600,000 displaced persons were camping on the outskirts of the capital.

The situation degenerated rapidly during the 'democratic' period (1986–89) when the authorities embarked on a policy based on *the use of tribal militia and famine as arms of warfare*. Taking advantage of traditional hostility between one group of Arab-speaking nomads, the 'Baggaras', and the Dinkas, who made up the largest battalions of the rebellion, the government armed the Baggaras and gave them total freedom to 'fight the SPLA', in other words to massacre Dinka civilians. Grouped in the 'Murahaleen' militia, the Baggaras committed much violence, even capturing survivors, particularly women and children, to sell them as slaves in the north. At the same time, playing on the ethnic antagonism among southerners, the Khartoum government established militia groups in tribes hostile to the Dinkas, such as some of the Nuer clans, the Mundari, the Murle or the Toposa clans. The exactions of these militia groups met with equal violence from the guerrillas and led the population to flee en masse from the country towards the towns, which soon became crammed with totally dependent refugees.

In 1988, the 'terrible year', a combination of drought, floods and an invasion of locusts which annihilated the rest of the crops, ended in terrible famine. Militia activity doubled while the government hindered the convoys of aid sent to the threatened regions. In rural areas, droves of starving refugees, hunted down by militiamen who stole their remaining livestock and rags, headed towards the towns in search of the food that the government would not give them. Their hopes were often disappointed. To escape summary execution by the militia or the regular army on the hunt for 'SPLA fighters', young boys often preferred embarking on a long journey towards Ethiopia – from 600 to 1000 km on foot – in which a third were to die on the way. In autumn 1988, the refugee camps of Itang and Fugnido in the Ethiopian province of Illubabor sheltered nearly 400,000 people, fed to the best of their ability by UNHCR relief workers. Inside the country, there were hundreds of thousands of displaced persons and about a million and a half people had ended up around Khartoum. In the worst camps in the provinces, the mortality rate was appalling: at Abyei, Meiram or Torit, the death rate reached

Operation Lifeline Sudan

The misadventures of the UN Operation Lifeline Sudan serve as an example of the helplessness of relief agencies faced with a regime firmly decided to reach its political goals whatever the cost in human lives.

Following the 1988 famine, under pressure from international NGOs, the Sudanese government accepted the principle of a United Nations emergency operation to help all the threatened populations, including those in the areas controlled by guerrillas. This agreement, signed in April 1989, was then hailed as an unprecedented breakthrough of humanitarian principles in a conflict known for its extreme brutality. In 1989–90 Lifeline I allowed 90,000 tonnes of food to be sent into the worst affected regions. However, from 1990 onwards the new government in power, as a result of the coup on 1 July 1989, did its level best to hinder the pursuit of emergency aid operations in the areas it did not control: in 1990–91, Lifeline II was unable to send more than half the aid supplied during the previous year and the operation could not really be resumed in 1992.

The reasons for this failure are mainly political and ideological: for the Sudanese authorities, Lifeline was an unacceptable violation of its sovereignty and a gesture of support for the rebellion. Also, the basic principles of this humanitarian operation were in total contradiction with the logic of a regime committed to massive social transformation, using massacre, food as a weapon and forced displacement of the population to modify the ethnic and religious landscape of the country.

Because it did not understand the true nature of the new regime soon enough, the United Nations found itself exhausted by this obstacle course without ever having been able to bring sufficient aid to the threatened population. It is now at a dead end and the Sudanese people at risk are more than ever out of reach of international aid.

over four times that of the Korem camp in Ethiopia which had shaken public opinion in 1984. But the Sudanese tragedy did not trigger the same movement of solidarity and by the end of 1988, 250,000 people had died in general indifference. The following year, the United Nations set up a vast relief programme, 'Operation Lifeline Sudan', at a time when a negotiated solution to the conflict seemed likely. The process came to an abrupt end when the Moslem extremists of the Islamic National Front (INF) seized power in a coup during the night of 1 July 1989.

The new INF government stepped up the war into another stage of *mass deportation of civilians*. Previous practices were not however abandoned – the tribal militia were given official recognition by the Popular Defence Act of 6 November 1989 and carried on their operations in a more organized and military manner, but just as savagely. As

Kala Azar

Visceral Leishmaniosis, or kala-azar, is a parasitic disease transmitted by a sand fly. Fever, severe weight loss and swelling of the spleen are the main clinical signs of this disease which kills in only a few months, but is usually confined to small endemic outbreaks.

The west of the Sudanese province of Upper Nile was more or less free from this disease until 1984, when an unprecented epidemic broke out in the wake of the civil war. Since then the disease has affected tens of thousands of victims – 50,000 perhaps out of an estimated population of 300,000 to 700,000 people in the areas that have been worst affected by the fighting. In some villages, 40 per cent of the people have been wiped out.

In southern Sudan, kala-azar has actually fed on the civil war and displacements of population. Difficult access and widespread fighting are a permanent threat that hinders any large-scale medical action. No proper control of the endemic sources is really possible in the current climate of insecurity in the region, and the disease continues to spread towards the north and south.

The Sudanese government hinders any effective control of the disease: the authorities do not consider kala-azar, which strikes mainly the southern population, as a threat to public health. The relief agencies have been refused access to government-controlled zones.

Yet again, fighting the epidemic comes down to the crucial problem of access to victims. The international community appears to be paralysed, both for medical action and for food aid. The World Health Organization holds neither the mandate nor the power to intervene, as the Sudanese government continues to deny the importance of the problem. Without emergency measures of treatment and control of the disease, kala-azar will again claim tens of thousands of 'casualties of war'.

---

for the food 'weapon', it once again hit the headlines when Operation Lifeline was scuttled in 1990 by the joint effects of the Khartoum government's hostility and the weakness of the United Nations, which was keen to treat the new government tactfully. But Khartoum's latest 'innovation' was the launch of clean-up operations in zones considered sensitive, particularly around the capital. INF activists attacked the shanty towns, bulldozed them and transferred the Khartoum refugees by force to camps in the middle of the desert where nothing was ready to shelter them. Parked in camps such as Dar es Salam, west of Omdurman, or Jebel Awlia, 40 km south of Khartoum, unable to earn a living far from the capital, these Christian and Animist displaced persons are totally at the mercy of Islamic organizations. In one year, over 500,000 people were displaced and the programme seems to be keeping its pace, to the relief of the INF leaders, who considered the Khartoum refugees, most of them from the south, as a support base for the SPLA. Other deportation operations are currently under way in the western provinces, Darfour and above all the south of Kordofan: they were launched as a response to the SPLA's attempts to penetrate these regions populated by black Moslems. The spectre of a generalized black African uprising with the participation of the black Moslems haunted the 'Arab' elite after the fighting in the Nouba mountains in 1989 and in Darfour the following year. The reaction was brutal. In Darfour in January 1992, the Daoud Bolad uprising was crushed at the cost of 3000 lives and 100,000 displaced persons, whereas the Nouba mountains were the scene of a more global and systematic policy of resettlement of the Nouba black Africans in the region of El Obeid, populated with Arabs, to make way for large groups of Baggaras settling on their land. By June 1992, 25,000 people had been deported and 31,000 were waiting in the transit camp of Kadugli in a situation of extreme precariousness, under army surveillance.

A new element was added to these government policies: *the implosion of the SPLA led to the flight of the civilians placed under its administration.* At the peak of its power, at the beginning of 1990, the SPLA controlled over 500,000 km^2 in southern Sudan and its authority extended over the refugee – and training – camps in Ethiopia where 400,000 people lived. Following the fall of the Mengistu regime in Ethiopia in May 1991, various groups of Ethiopian rebels, who had collaborated with the Khartoum government to overthrow the Ethiopian government, attacked the camps. Masses of refugees flowed across the frontier in a state of confusion and extreme distress. The loss of the Ethiopian 'sanctuaries' and the following mayhem provoked a major division within the SPLA in August 1991. In October, the secessionists, mainly Nuers and Shilluks, allied with a pro-governmental militia of the same ethnic origin, swooped down on the Bor region, peopled with Dinkas, killing men, women and children, stealing the livestock and setting fire to grain stocks. The shock was enormous and hundreds of thousands of refugees fled towards the south to escape the massacre. Not long afterwards, in February 1992, with 400 million dollars' worth of arms paid for by its new ally, Iran, the government launched a large-scale offensive and seized most of the guerrilla strongholds in no more than four months. The former refugees in Ethiopia, now back in Sudan fleeing from the militias' exactions, were therefore pushed back to the borders or caught up in the war. In June 1992, 85,000 of them had fled to Uganda and 22,000 to Kenya; 150,000 hesitated at the border while nearly 500,000 displaced persons wandered around the countryside, trapped by the fighting.

The only food aid that still gets to southern Sudan, supplied by the United Nations World Food Programme (WFP) operating from Uganda, is not sufficient to feed all these displaced persons. Were these refugees to cross the borders, the UNHCR clearly could not cope, as its means are already stretched to the limit by other disasters: 35,000

Zairean refugees in Uganda and nearly 400,000 refugees from Ethiopia and Somalia in the north of Kenya by the end of June 1992. Moreover, some United Nations agencies such as UNICEF, which sends relief supplies to the camps where Khartoum's displaced persons have been forcibly transferred, practise a policy of tactful understanding towards the government which raises many questions about their real aims. As to independent humanitarian organizations, they are left powerless by the government's determination to bar all access to the populations in the south. Neither can they bring aid to any displaced persons either in Darfour, in south Kordofan or even around Khartoum, where the population gathered in the middle of the desert is totally dependent on the aid provided by Islamic organizations, the only ones authorized to work in the camps. In Sudan, scope for humanitarian action is shrinking dramatically and relief agencies have lost all access to the most threatened populations.

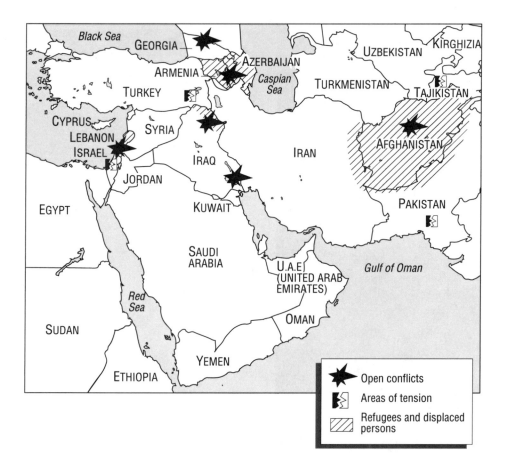

Open conflicts

Areas of tension

Refugees and displaced persons

Middle East

Introduction

Far from solving the problems of the Middle East, the breaking up of the Soviet Union and the Gulf War appear to have exacerbated the latent conflicts between communities, ethnic groups and states and thus the danger faced by populations. Three regions give particular cause for worry: the Caucasus, the Near East and Central Asia.

In the Caucasus, with the collapse of communism went the slab of lead which, for decades, covered latent tensions and conflicts between neighbours so that nationalistic claims thought to be forgotten have risen to the surface with uncanny speed. The region caught fire as early as 1988. Even before the fall of Mikhail Gorbachev, Armenia and Azerbaijan clashed over Nagorno-Karabakh in a war which has already caused the death of over two thousand civilians. Since 1992, the conflict has spread to Armenia and Azerbaijan themselves.

Still in the Caucasus, the war between the Georgians and the Ossets has been going on since 1989. Under the Soviet Union, this area was divided so that North Ossetia (600,000 inhabitants) was part of the Russian Federation and South Ossetia (100,000 inhabitants) was part of Georgia. Since 1925, the Ossets have been requesting their reunification. Faced with the nationalist effervescence in Georgia, South Ossetia rose in 1989 and in 1990 elected its own parliament. The Georgians reacted by cancelling the autonomous status of South Ossetia. In December 1991, the break was made complete by the proclamation of an independent republic of South Ossetia. In spite of the agreement signed on 24 June 1992 by Eduard Shevardnadze, president of the Georgian State Council, and the Russian president, Boris Yeltsin, war kept going, and has caused about a thousand deaths since 1990, as well as 1500 wounded and about 100,000 displaced persons on the Ossetian side alone. Current clashes in Abkhazia have further increased tension between Georgians and the people of the northern Caucasus.

A little further south, in the Near East, the Gulf War has thrown into sharp relief a number of unsolved problems. The euphoria of the liberation of Kuwait and the promises – which were not kept – of democratization distracted attention from the excesses committed by the Kuwaiti authorities once they had returned to their country. The first victims were the 400,000 Palestinians who lived in the Emirate before the Gulf War. Suspected of having collaborated with the Iraqis, today they have to face reprisals and harassment from the authorities. Only 100,000 are still in Kuwait in 1992.

The Palestinians are also the target of Israeli repression, notably inthe West Bank and the Gaza Strip. Since the start of the Intifada in the Occupied Territories in December 1987, the Israeli authorities have hardened their attitude towards the Palestinians of the interior. Houses are demolished, people expelled to Jordan and Lebanon or thrown into prison in an arbitrary fashion. The arrival in power of the Labour government in June 1992 and the partial freezing of Israeli colonization of the Occupied Territories may cause the situation to change and relaunch the peace process.

Southern Lebanon continues to suffer from the effects of the un-declared war between Israel and certain Palestinian or Lebanese groups. For more than 20 years now, the population of the south of the country has lived in precarious and violent circumstances, bearing the full brunt of the backlash of the fighting and reprisals from the Israeli army and air force.

In Central Asia, the collapse of the Soviet Union could have explosive effects.The political legitimacy of the four new states in the region – Uzbekistan, Tajikistan, Turkmenistan, Kirghizia – is based on ethnic nationalism. But the region is made up of various closely linked ethnic groups, and the cities host large Russian and European communities. In the wake of independence, whole populations have been displaced because of their ethnic allegiance: the Uzbeks are leaving Tajikistan for Uzbekistan, the Tajiks of Uzbekistan are forcibly assimilated and Asia's Russians, Jews and Germans are fleeing towards Moscow, Israel or Germany.

In Afghanistan, the taking of Kabul by the Mujahedin rebels has not been enough to bring back peace. A violent civil war has broken out pitting the Tajiks, the Uzbeks and the Shi'ites against the Pashtuns of Gulbuddin Hekmatyar. While Afghan refugees can be seen returning from their 10-year exile in Pakistan, the people of Kabul are trying to flee the fighting in the capital. Now that the united struggle against Soviet occupation has given way to ethnic animosities, there are fears that large-scale displacements of populations within the country are yet to come.

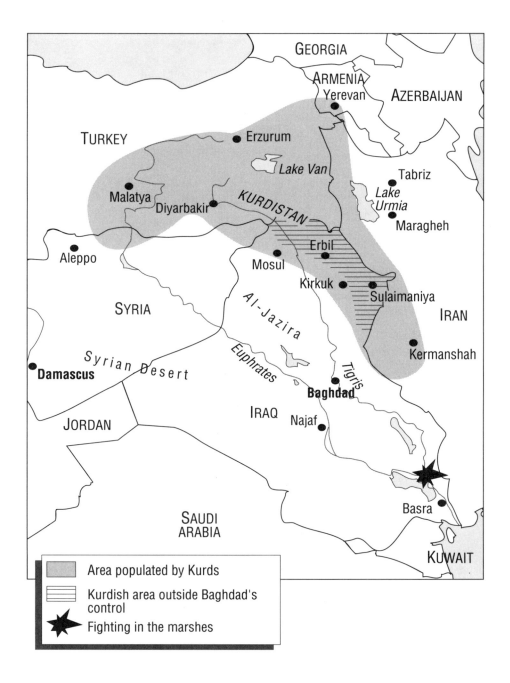

Area populated by Kurds

Kurdish area outside Baghdad's control

Fighting in the marshes

IRAQ

The Iraqi regime is still in power after what was in theory its humiliating defeat by the United Nations coalition forces. The fierce repression after the uprisings in the Shia Moslem south and the Kurdish north in March 1991 allowed Saddam Hussein's regime to tighten its hold on a large part of the country. Flouting United Nations Security Council resolution 688, which expressly condemned the repression of civilian populations, the regime mercilessly tracks down the Shi'ites in the marshlands in the south-east of the country. In northern Iraq, 3.5 million Kurds enjoy a precarious de facto autonomy, in theory protected until December 1992 by a Western air umbrella.

The Kurds are paying dearly for this respite. Like other Iraqis, they are subject to the UN-imposed overall embargo on all supplies except food and medicines: this has caused a serious drop in living standards and the 17 million inhabitants of what was once one of the Arab world's richest countries have been reduced to meagre rations doled out by the government. To these restrictions – which do not apply, however, to the pillars of the regime such as the higher Baath party officials, members of the multifarious secret police corps and the Republican Guard elite – must be added the effects of a further embargo at home.

Since October 1991, Baghdad has effectively cut the Kurds' normal trade links with the rest of Iraq and imposed an internal blockade. Furthermore, this embargo is not merely economic: it entails actual military encirclement which only adds a feeling of insecurity to the impression of precariousness which is characteristic of this fragile 'free' area in the north of Iraq.

Resolution 688 and the right to intervene

Passed on 5 April 1991 during the most tense moments of the Kurdish exodus from Iraq, United Nations Security Council resolution 688 condemned the repression of the Iraqi civilian populations, demanded that Iraq put an end to the repression and insisted that humanitarian organizations have immediate accesss to the people at risk. It was the first time ever that the international community had so strongly denounced human rights violations in a sovereign country and so imperiously proclaimed the urgent need for humanitarian aid in the face of opposition from the government in question. This unprecedented resolution was hailed at the time as opening the way to a new era in international relations. In reality, it condemned repression of the Iraqi civilian population only insofar as the immense tide of refugees threatened peace and security in the region. This harked back to the traditional concept of international law based on the non-violation of frontiers and concern for stability.

It would be incorrect in theory and unwise in practice to think that the reaction of the international community in favour of the Kurds is likely to give rise to an international mechanism designed to protect populations in their own countries. The theory is wrong because the governments' intervention did not stem from a universal movement of solidarity but rather from a sense of their specific interests. And, in practical terms, any type of international protection is not dissuasive for long unless it involves a firm political commitment which is improbable, barring exceptional circumstances. Although defeated and placed under international surveillance, Iraq still provides a relevant illustration of the reticence shown by the Western countries when it comes to getting involved in internal crises. In April 1991, it took a feeling of responsibility on the part of the West in the face of the televised flight of an entire people over the borders. In the future, getting states to commit themselves to intervene will undoubtedly require a political interest, media visibility and the pressure of public opinion.

From intervention to indifference

When Shia Moslem and Kurdish Iraqis acted on the American call and rose against the Baghdad government in early March 1991, the Gulf War abruptly turned sour for the coalition still congratulating itself on its painless victory in liberating Kuwait from Iraqi occupation. The Republican Guards crushed the Shia uprising by mid-March while the coalition troops remained standing at ease on the sidelines, with the firm resolve not to get bogged down in Iraqi 'internal affairs'. At the same time, the Kurds rose in the northern towns, thinking that they were at last to free themselves from a 20-year dictatorship. The elation, however, was short-lived. Dangerously exposed outside their mountainous retreat, the ill-armed Kurds collapsed over the Easter weekend

The Kurdish question

The tragic repercussions of the Gulf War had to be felt before public opinion remembered the Kurdish problem. Twenty-five million Kurds live spreadeagled between five states: Iraq (5 million), Iran (6 million), Turkey (12 million), Syria and the former Soviet Union.

For more than a century, Kurdish aspirations to independence have been a long story of hopes and missed opportunities. The 1920 Treaty of Sevres, which acknowledged their right to autonomy and, eventually, to independence, was never applied. Since then, Kurds have taken up arms in Iraq, Iran and Turkey to gain their independence but, far from turning state rivalry to their advantage, they have frequently been used by those governments to serve state interests.

Thus in Iraq, the Kurds rose with the support of Iran after the government had called into question the autonomy agreement signed on 11 March 1970, before being sacrificed on the altar of Iraq-Iran reconciliation as part of the Algiers agreement of March 1975. In the same manner, the Kurds were used by both parties during the Iraq-Iran war to weaken the enemy and were then subjected to severe repression at the end of the conflict, notably in Halabja, Iraq, in March 1988.

However, Iraq is not the only country where the Kurds are oppressed. In Iran, where they rose in 1979, their fight for autonomy was crushed by Khomeini's Guardians of the Revolution. And the Kurdish question in Turkey has been taboo since the early days of the republic. For several decades, the Kurds did not exist officially and did not have the right to speak their language. For a few months now, the beginning of a change has been observed, but the government has not managed to engage in talks with the Kurdish Workers' Party (PKK) which has been fighting for independence since 1984. In the south-east of the country, the civilian population is more than ever caught in the endless cycle of terrorism and repression.

before a tank-and-artillery Iraqi counter-offensive. Here began the most brutal exodus of modern history. In incredible disorder, on roads crowded with columns of refugees under fire from helicopter gunships, more than two million Kurds headed for the Turkish and Iranian borders rather than risk the wrath of a regime which in a matter of years had razed 4000 of their villages, repeatedly used poison gas against the civilian population and caused as many as 180,000 of their number to 'disappear'.

Fearing the breakup of Iraq and destabilization of the region, the coalition countries let repression run its course. But television coverage of wretched Kurds dying in freezing mountain weather day after day aroused huge sympathy from international public opinion. Washington's allies in Paris, London and other Western capitals brought rising pressure on the White House. This was especially the case with Turkey which – since the start of the exodus – had done everything in its power to keep the refugees in the mountains, beyond the Turkish border, and intended at all costs to avoid the overspill of hundreds of thousands of Iraqi Kurds into the south-east of its territory, which was already the scene of a merciless struggle between the army and the Turkish Kurd 'separatists'.

So came Security Council resolution 688 and the Western intervention designed to keep Iraqi Kurds inside Iraq by creating what became known as 'safe havens' temporarily protected by coalition troops. Thus was born Operation Provide Comfort, which at one point involved more than 20,000 coalition troops from a dozen countries.

This intervention did in fact make it possible to supply vital aid to the refugees in distress but left in suspense the crucial question of the long-term protection of Kurds after their return to Iraq. Billed as a 'humanitarian exercise to resettle and protect the Kurds', in fact Provide Comfort was conceived as a quick in-and-out operation to persuade fearful Kurds to return to their homes in a relatively small triangular area along the Iraqi-Syrian-Turkish borders. Within days thousands of refugees left the mountains for home. That movement prompted a similar reflux from Iran by more than a million Iraqi Kurds who had taken refuge in Iran. From this point on, the main aim of the coalition troops was to pack up and leave without even obtaining a political settlement, the negotiations with Baghdad on the autonomy of Kurdistan having failed. Air cover was provided and on 15 July 1991, the last land forces went back across the Turkish border promising the disillusioned Kurds that 'help was just a telephone call away'.

In fact tens of thousands of Iraqi Kurds camped out in tents on the mountains and plains rather than return to cities under Iraqi control. Only when Kurdish guerrillas subsequently pushed Iraqi soldiers and police out of Erbil and Sulaimaniya did most of the population return. Iraqi Kurds still live on the edge, ready to flee to the borders at the slightest sign of a major offensive by Baghdad. Renewed but limited fighting in October 1991 sent more than 100,000 resettled Kurds scurrying to hastily construct tent camps in the hills. There they joined hundreds of thousands of homeless Kurds, many of them from Kirkuk.

But as long as international attention continues to be focused on Iraq, the discreet, tried-and-tested methods of repression will probably be preferred to military reconquest. In the meantime, the Baghdad regime merely steps up the pressure using military encirclement and a stringent internal embargo which deprives the Kurdish area of the means needed to run a normal administration and causes serious shortages. Deprived of food and, above all, of fuel for heating during the worst winter in 40 years, the Kurds are still heavily dependent on international assistance. To make things worse, they were also powerless to stop the departure in July 1992 of all but a handful of international organizations, the eyes and ears of an increasingly distant outside world.

The door closes again

In the wake of the Gulf War, Baghdad had no choice but to accept the Memorandum of Understanding put to them by the United Nations for setting up a vast humanitarian operation designed to assist the civilian populations and particularly the displaced persons. But from the MOU's signature on 17 April 1991, it was clear that Baghdad would not tolerate for long this international presence which was perceived as an unacceptable violation of Iraqi sovereignty.

Even before the last coalition troops left Iraqi soil, Baghdad began testing UN resolve. It started with the sensitive question of the embargo: obviously exaggerated ma nutrition and infant mortality figures were produced, which UNICEF – probably in an attempt to keep up relations with the government – agreed to publish and endorse. The next step was to hinder the work of the humanitarian organizations in every way possible. As the months went by, the chances of obtaining visas or permits to travel round the country dwindled while organizations bringing aid were viewed with increasing suspicion. In any event, the United Nations never obtained access – even to carry out a short survey – in the southern marshlands to monitor treatment of Shia Moslems subjected to appalling repression. The UN was also powerless to protect the refugees who had been repatriated to the regions controlled by Baghdad.

With Iraq refusing to extend the MOU beyond 1 July 1992, the United Nations found itself increasingly isolated and the few remaining humanitarian organizations have become a prime target. Baghdad will stop at nothing to get rid of embarrassing witnesses. In a matter of weeks in the summer of 1992, a series of attacks occurred which made it clear to the United Nations and to the humanitarian organizations that their presence was no longer tolerated in Iraq. Only determination of the international community can prevent the door closing on northern Iraq for good.

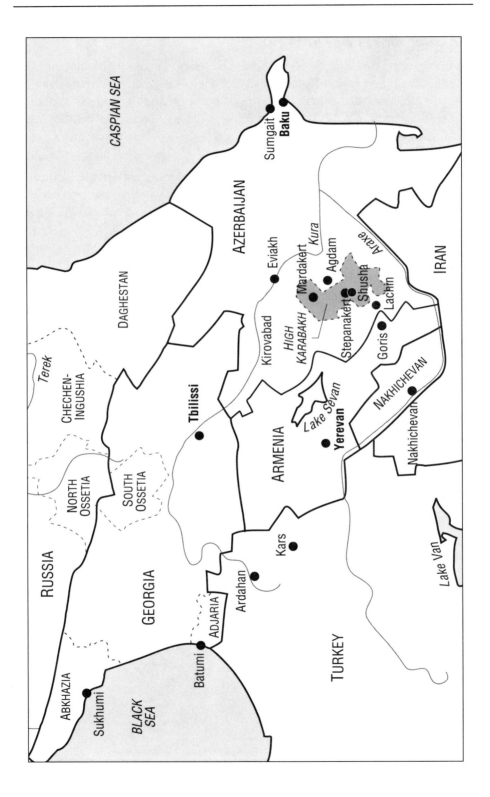

NAGORNO-KARABAKH

The nationality crisis which had been smouldering for many years in the Soviet Union did not wait for the fall of the empire in the autumn of 1991 to break out openly in the Caucusus, more precisely in Nagorno-Karabakh. This small mountainous territory – 4400 km^2 – and its 190,000 inhabitants, 80 per cent of whom are Armenians, is enclaved in the Republic of Azerbaijan and separated from the Republic of Armenia by a narrow strip of land.

This conflict, with its tragic and complex historical roots, has taken a terrible toll. Thousands have been killed in both communities, refugees number hundreds of thousands (Azerbaijanis expelled from Armenia, Armenians driven out of Azerbaijan), both economies have been ruined and the civilians are the first victims.

A tragic and complex history

No sooner had the two republics obtained their independence in 1919 than Nagorno-Karabakh, which had been snatched from the Persian empire by Russia, became the hub of an Armenian-Azerbaijani war. In 1923, three years after Sovietization, Moscow ignored requests from Yerevan and decided in favour of Baku. Nagorno-Karabakh was to be an autonomous region within Azerbaijan. This 'autonomy', however, was a fiction for the political, cultural and religious rights of the Armenians were not respected. Large-scale population transfers made the two republics 'homogeneous'. Little by little Armenians left Nakhichevan where they made up more than half the population, whereas 100,000 Azerbaijanis were forced to leave Armenia in 1948 to make room for a major wave of 'repatriates'.

After decades of silence and oppression, perestroika made it possible to express discontent and protest. On 20 February 1988, the parliament of Nagorno-Karabakh officially requested reunification of the region with Armenia. But the anti-Armenian pogrom that followed at Soumgait on 27 and 28 February was considered by many in Armenia as the answer from Baku.

A few weeks later, Moscow refused to grant Armenian claims. The conflict rapidly gathered momentum to escape from central control and spread beyond the borders of Karabakh. The civilian inhabitants of both republics from then on bore the full brunt of the consequences of the war in the form of pogroms, attacks, surges of hate and forced transfers of population.

From the beginning of 1988 on, thousands of Azerbaijanis fled from Armenia, victims of pressure, brutalities or the wave of panic which swept through their community. By the end of 1988, 170,000 of them had left the country. The Armenians of Azerbaijan fled in the other direction so that 400,000 people moved to Armenia. At the beginning of 1990, the last Armenian families fled Baku in the face of pogroms. In spring of 1991, several thousand Armenian villagers were deported in turn from Nagorno Karabakh to Armenia by Soviet troops.

The spread of war

The situation got even worse after the independence of both Armenia and Azerbaijan was proclaimed. At the end of 1991, Azerbaijan put an end to Nagorno-Karabakh's status of autonomy and the enclave announced its independence. Attempts at mediation were fruitless and the fighting, far from dying down, grew to become a war in its own right equipped with the weapons handed over to the republics by the Soviet army.

Since the taking of Shusha on 8 May 1992, Stepanakert, the capital of Nagorno-Karabakh, no longer has to live in fear of the Grad missiles launched from the town on the surrounding hills. But the traumatized population has been further frightened by the regular use by the Azerbaijani forces of Sukhoi 25 bombers since the beginning of July. After six months of intensive shelling, of which the hospital was a prime target, Stepanakert, which had a population of 57,000 at the start of 1989, mourns its dead by the hundred and is now almost totally in ruins. Those who have not fled to the surrounding villages are housed in makeshift shelters after having learnt to survive in cellars. In a conflict in which one can only guess at the numbers of dead and refugees, it is extremely difficult to estimate the present population of Stepanakert. This task is made harder by the fact that the authorities of the newly created Republic of Nagorno-Karabakh, after having long opposed the departure of civilians for Armenia, 'so as not to depopulate Artsakh', appear now to allow women and children to join families and friends there. The taking of Lachin by Armenian forces in mid-May achieved its objective, which was to prise open the barrier which separated Nagorno-Karabakh from Armenia and break the enclave's isolation.

The health situation continues to be extremely precarious. After a severe winter made worse by the absence of electricity and shortages which spare no sectors of a totally-devastated economy, the people have seen no improvement in their living conditions apart from the appearance of fresh foodstuffs. In most cases they lack even the most basic medical supplies but must endure the repeated shelling of enemy artillery, in particular since the Azerbaijani offensive of June 1992. Many towns are affected, in the north, where the Baku troops have succeeded in getting a hold in the Mardakert region, but also to the east, where the Martuni hospital has been subjected to violent artillery shelling. Thirty thousand refugees have fled from the combat zone, in particular towards Stepanakert.

For the Azerbaijanis, the year 1992 marks the spread of a war which up to now had relatively spared them. Well before it fell, Shusha had become a ghost town, whose population had fallen from 20,000 to 4000 as a result of shelling. The taking of Khodjaly (a few kilometres north of Stepanakert) by Armenian fighters on 25 and 26 February 1992 caused a shockwave which had wide political implications in the Azerbaijan Republic. More important than the humiliation of the military defeat, public opinion in Azerbaijan was deeply shocked by the conditions of the taking of this town which had 6300 inhabitants in 1991 (2100 in 1988), a majority of whom were refugees. The exactions committed against the civilian population and the large number of victims (200 were killed according to the Azerbaijanis and a number of neutral observers) made Khodjaly a symbol. Violence continued to escalate with the spring offensive launched by the Armenians during which acts of cruelty and pillage became legion in the towns captured. The conflict no longer spares those living in the regions surrounding Karabakh. A few miles from the front line, Agdam has undergone several deadly bombardments and has become a refuge for the people of Khodjaly and the surrounding countryside.

Even if the food and health situation of Azerbaijan may seem relatively positive (contrary to Armenia and even more, Nagorno-Karabakh, this country is not facing a blockade) the republic is up against many difficulties such as a chronic shortage of medical supplies and equipment, damaged hospitals and difficulties in coping with refugees.

The problem of the refugees is one of the most serious the republics have to face. Armenia, which has not yet surmounted the consequences of the December 1988 earthquake, does not have the means to take in all those who have fled from Azerbaijan. Many, particularly city dwellers with qualifications, have found refuge in Russia if only under conditions which are often extremely precarious. In Azerbaijan, the 'Eraz' or refugees from Armenia, who are mostly of rural origin, have joined the hundreds of thousands of unemployed (from 700,000 to one million in 1992). Treated as outcasts by a society which sees them as foreigners, in their desperation they are easy prey for manipulation. In 1988 and January 1990, they formed the vanguard in the anti-Armenian pogroms and now support the radicals.

The continuation of the war brings with it its store of dangers for the civilian population.

In this conflict which is rooted in a tragic history and carried out against a backdrop of passionate allegiance, the humanitarian organizations have the greatest difficulty in persuading the belligerents to comply with certain basic principles such as refraining from attacking structures marked with the Red Cross sign, protecting civilians or distributing aid on all sides without discrimination. In spite of all their efforts, hospitals are regularly bombarded – sometimes deliberately – it has never been possible to ensure regular delivery of supplies to needy groups across the lines and the civilians are the prime victims of a war which with each passing day locks them even tighter into an endless sequence of hate, bitterness and vengeance.

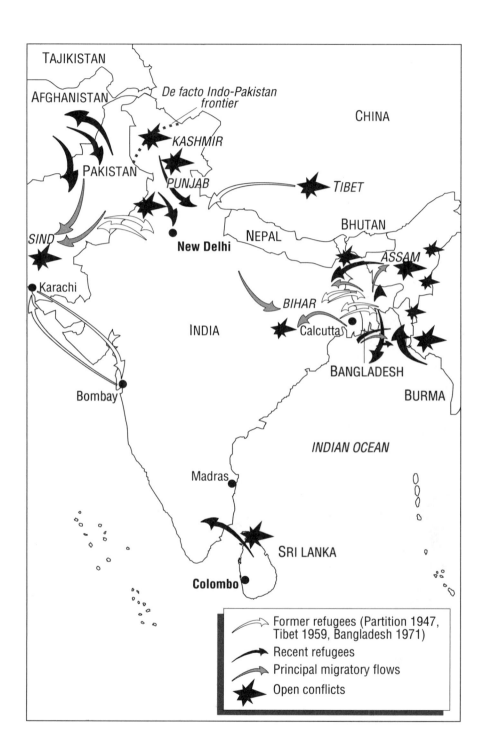

Former refugees (Partition 1947, Tibet 1959, Bangladesh 1971)

Recent refugees

Principal migratory flows

Open conflicts

South asia

Introduction

India, Pakistan, Bangladesh, Sri Lanka and even Bhutan are torn by centrifugal forces waving the flags of ethnic identity, regionalism, autonomy and even independence. Governments respond with complex political ploys, in turn redistributing wealth and using force. Guerrilla movements and their rival factions use armed struggle to express their disapproval of modern states, which are seen as predators or colonialists. Civilian populations bear the heavy brunt of the 'rebel' groups' terrorism and the blind reprisals of the army and police.

In south Asia, with its billion people, the present crises are the legacy of a lengthy past: first, the frontiers, drawn up during the British colonial era, that included non-native racial groups on the fringes of the empire; secondly, the partition between Moslem Pakistan and India, which led to countless massacres and the most extensive forced migrations of modern history in 1947. These dramatic events have been carried over into the present. The current situation of Kashmir and the bloody birth of Bangladesh 20 years ago are proof of the after-effects of Partition. Furthermore, the unity of states in the region is threatened by tensions due to ethnic, linguistic, religious, social and economic diversity. Conflicts in south Asia, while of widely varying types, are basically linked to four kinds of problem.

Minorities which have been forcibly integrated into modern states

The case of north-east India and the Chittagong Hill Tracts has points in common with the situation in Tibet. In Bangladesh, demographic pressure in the lowlands together with economic opportunities in the highlands is leading the Bengalis to settle en masse in the tribal regions. The 'Shanti Bahini' or Peace Corps of the Chittagong Hill Tracts, run by the tribal groups, have risen to halt immigration and win the right to live on their lands in their traditional lifestyle. The region, under the occupation of the Bangladeshi army, is often the scene of violence by the paramilitary forces, which sometimes results in large-scale massacres. In India, the army is stationed in the five small northeastern states which border Burma.

Moslem Kashmir united with India

Since 1947, neither the three wars between India and Pakistan, nor the UN resolutions nor negotiations between Pakistan and India have succeeded in settling the fate of the Kashmiris. Since 1989, this state has been the scene of a multidirectional armed separatist insurrection which, in turn, has been met with the direct intervention of New Delhi, the suppression of civil liberties and repression by the army and police.

The claims of the 'Sons of the Soil'

The frustrations of the Indian Assamese and the Pakistani Sindhis, numerically and economically dominated by refugees and immigrants, have burst into violence. The open crisis in Assam began in 1979. The holding of elections was prevented by massacres of civilians in 1983 and failure to reach a negotiated solution. New Delhi stepped in, the state was occupied by the army and the 'foreign' population fled. In Sind, the Sindhis felt dispossessed by the rising economic influence of the Mohajirs, Moslem refugees who had come to Karachi at the time of partition, and by the arrival in the province of hundreds of thousands of immigrants in search of land and job opportunities. The Sindhi resentment soon turned into an open crisis. With the war in Afghanistan, tension became extreme as political institutions became further discredited, urban guerrilla warfare broke out in Karachi and Hyderabad and crime, kidnapping and arms and drug trafficking were rife.

Separatist movements

In the Punjab, Bihar and Sri Lanka, deep-rooted regionalist tensions have hardened into separatist radicalism. The movements of the wealthy in the Indian Punjab for an independent 'Khalistan' were toughened by the rise of Sikh fundamentalism. In spite of elections in 1992, the Punjab is being won over by violence and Hindu civilians are fleeing Sikh terrorism. In southern Bihar, the movement of the poor, 'Jharkhand Mukti Morcha', is claiming a 'Jharkhand', a land of the people of the forest, for the tribal populations, while calling for effective economic measures. In Sri Lanka, the war waged by the Tamil guerrillas for the creation of an independent state in the north and east of the island is dragging the whole country into an escalation of violence.

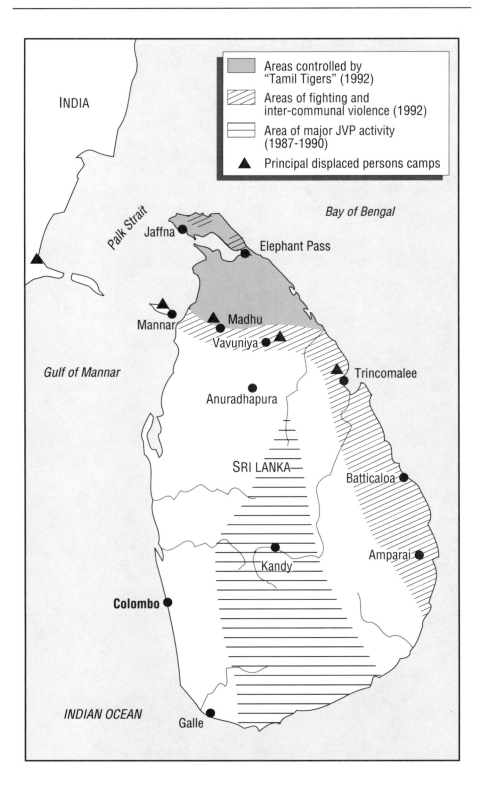

SRI LANKA

On the world map of violent situations, Sri Lanka stands out because of the concatenation and overlapping of long-standing conflicts. For a small country with 17 million inhabitants, which had enjoyed a quality of life without equal in south Asia, the human cost is enormous. More than 50,000 are dead or missing, most of them civilians, almost 600,000 people are displaced within the country, the 200,000 and more refugees in India are threatened with forced repatriation and there are several hundred thousand expatriates scattered throughout the world.

Violence breeds violence

Since the 1970s, Sri Lanka has been suffering from an overall crisis which calls into question the structures inherited from the colonial period. The claims for independence of the Tamil minority in the north served as a detonator, but questioning of the regime had already begun in 1971 with a revolt of the Sinhalese youth. The deep-seated causes of the crisis are the contradictions between a crippled economy and an advanced social policy which ensured peace up until the 1970s, but which became increasingly costly as the population grew. The large number of educated young people suffering from underemployment was the decisive weight which threw the social system out of balance. As a result, and on account of the shortsightedness of the ruling class, insecurity spread thoughout society. Every new step taken in the scale of violence added a new category to the list of potential victims and the circle of violence widened, geographically and socially.

As early as in 1958 and up to 1977, intermittent incidents occurred between the Sinhalese majority and the Tamil minority in the east-central rice-growing colonies, the

Refugees and repatriates: pawns of political strategies?

At the end of May 1992, the island had 573,000 displaced persons to which must be added about 200,000 refugees in India, including 80,000 in more than 200 camps, not to mention 200,000 refugees in Western countries. In all, the conflicts in Sri Lanka have generated almost a million refugees and displaced persons.

An initial wave of refugees to India in 1983 was made up of Tamil people from the cities who were joined from 1985 by fishermen and poor farmers from the combat zones. The intervention of India in 1987 – which was presented as guaranteeing the restoration of law and order in Sri Lanka – went hand in hand with a first wave of repatriation, with the UNHCR unable to control the process on Indian territory.

When fighting resumed in June 1990, these repatriates left again. To restrain the flow, the UNHCR set up 'open relief centres' not only to accommodate the inhabitants temporarily during the bursts of fighting but also to dissuade those wishing to leave and to provide shelter for the repatriates. Initially presented as an experiment designed to test the possibility of stemming refugee movements by acting at the source, the project was offset from the start by the will of both the Indian and Sri Lankan governments to encourage, and even to force, refugees in Indian camps to return home, as they had become undesirable after the assassination of Rajiv Gandhi.

At the end of June 1992, 23,000 people had returned and a further 80,000 had been planned in order to empty the Indian camps. Although it timidly spoke out against repatriation, the UNHCR appears to be backing a process over which it has no control. Its stance has been met with severe criticism from humanitarian organizations, which stress the impossibility of ascertaining whether such returns are voluntary, the difficulty in providing genuine protection for the repatriates and the political nature of the operation, as India and the West appear to be keener to get rid of the refugees than to ensure their protection.

central plantation regions and the capital. At the same time the educated Tamils, considering that they were victims of discriminatory measures, began to espouse separatist feelings. After 1977, and particulary after 1983, politically manipulated violence worsened and some Tamils moved to the east and north where they were in the majority.

From 1981 in the north and 1985 in the east, the development of a Tamil guerrilla movement triggered repression from 1981 to 1987 on the part of the Colombo government, from 1987 to 1990 by Indian peacekeeping troops and since 1990 again

The Eastern Province: a logic of civil war

Communities in this area are mixed – 43 per cent Tamils, 32 per cent Moslems, 25 per cent Sinhalese in 1981. In the semi-urban coastal fringe Tamil and Moslem towns have coexisted for centuries. The hinterland was more recently populated by Moslem or Tamil immigrants and by Sinhalese settlers.

The civil war began after 1985, when the LTTE, originally based in the north, attempted to impose their rule to the detriment of other Tamil groups, to open a second front and reach their objective of an 'Eelam' made up of the north and east of the island. When fighting resumed between the LTTE and the Sri Lankan army in June 1990, hundreds of thousands of people fled. The Sinhalese settlers and the local Tamils and Moslems became pawns in a strategy designed to manipulate and heighten inter-communal tensions in order to cause the unwanted to flee and thus to gain ground. The army's special units have repeatedly engaged in violence. The LTTE force the Tamils to support them and drive out those Moslems who do not profer such support. The government forces have armed Sinhalese and Moslem self-defence militia. The dissuasion effect is non-existent, but the move provides maximum encouragement to carry out reprisals. Attacks on villages, buses, country markets and even mosques are common occurrences and civilian victims can be counted in thousands.

The violence which wiped out three villages on 28 and 29 April 1992 is a tragic illustration of this logic of civil war. Muthugala and Karapola were Tamil villages, Alanchipotana was Moslem. The LTTE attacked Alanchipotana at night and massacred everybody they found. At dawn, the Moslems took revenge on Muthugala and Karapola. The massacres took a toll of 170 victims, half of them children. The traumatized survivors live in terror or have left to swell the ranks of the refugee camps on the coast.

by Sri Lankan forces. This has resulted in extensive population movements and widespread emigration to India and the West. Since 1986, the LTTE (Liberation Tigers of Tamil Eelam), the main guerrilla movement, has launched numerous attacks against Sinhalese and, later, Moslem civilians as well as against rival Tamil groups. This triggered a fresh flow of refugees, this time moving south.

In the south of the island, between 1987 and 1990, the JVP (People's Liberation Front), a Sinhalese revolutionary movement which was already active in 1971, took advantage of the intervention of India in the north-east to denounce the incompetence of the government. It carried out a spate of political assassinations before being savagely repressed by the armed forces and death squads. This again resulted in tens of thousands of dead and missing.

In a decade, a peaceful society has been transfigured by the toll of daily violence. Emergency laws have made the arbitrary the rule by preventing the courts from having any control over law and order operations. The use of force in the workings of society has become commonplace. The government has contributed to this by arming civilians to counter aggression from the insurrectional groups. By choosing a liberal economic system in 1977, it gave up its 'welfare state' role, thus losing part of its legitimacy and causing violent claims from fractional interests and poverty in the most vulnerable groups.

All negotiations undertaken over the last 10 years to find a solution to the conflict have failed. To internal violence was added interference from abroad. India, which has in turn supported and fought the Tamil guerrillas, has greatly contributed to the destabilization of the country. Since the assassination of Rajiv Gandhi in 1991, the Tamils of Sri Lanka have come under suspicion from the Indian authorities. Having lost their Indian 'back-up base', the LTTE are at present weakened but remain determined. The government of Sri Lanka is indecisive as to whether to seek a political solution or continue the fighting now raging in the north of the island.

The history of the Sinhalese, Tamil and Moslem communities is that of long coexistence, until the concept of identity reappeared as a late import of Western views on ethnic allegiance and historic rights. The concept of territory suddenly took on obsessional importance. The Sinhalese see the entire island as a Buddhist 'sanctuary' threatened by Indian expansionism, whereas the Tamils want to defend their national home against Sinhalese and even Moslem expansionism. The impact of these beliefs in terms of human suffering is dramatic. Gaining control over a territory implies moving populations considered as having no historic right to be there, the resulting refugees then becoming a major element in the conflict.

Populations in danger

In the north under LTTE control and particularly in the Jaffna peninsula, the local people lack food and medical supplies, electricity and fuel oil, the more so since fighting began again in June 1990. Bombing and land attacks have claimed thousands of civilian victims. Nevertheless, the government has allowed the International Committee of the Red Cross (ICRC) to take food to Jaffna, and the hospitals continue to function under perilous conditions with the backing of humanitarian organizations. The LTTE tolerates the remains of a skeleton administration but enrols young people by force, demands exit visas, the cost of which prevents the poorest from leaving the region, and has expelled all Moslems after confiscating their property.

In the combat areas from Mannar to Batticaloa, civilians are subjected to a sequence of stress and respite. Those who could afford it have fled the region: Tamil fishermen have tried to reach India from Mannar and the Moslems have taken refuge in Colombo. The most needy take shelter permanently or intermittently in the camps opened by the

UNHCR in the heart of the danger zone, but even here, they are at the mercy of pressure from the LTTE and the army.

The countryside in the centre and south of the island has been the scene of violence on the part of the JVP, the army and the death squads. The numbers of victims run into tens of thousands, particularly among young men of low caste. The police continue to fly in the face of human rights and refuse to release any information to the families of the missing. Twelve thousand proven cases of people 'going missing against their will' have been recorded by the UN group in charge of investigating such cases – the figure is the highest in the world. In addition, about 12,000 people are being held in prison.

The humanitarian implications

The violence which has ravaged Sri Lanka for more than 10 years has led to the disorganization of the state, the weakening of emergency services, emigration of qualified personnel – particularly in the medical field – a fall in welfare public spending and an increase in severe poverty. In the worst affected regions, humanitarian agencies are trying to run the health structures and to help the most threatened, particularly the refugees.

In Sri Lanka, as in any conflict, the room for manoeuvre of the humanitarian organizations is largely dependent on the acknowledgement by the belligerent parties of the neutrality and impartiality of their intervention. In Sri Lanka more than anywhere else, they have succeeded in convincing the parties in conflict and now command a genuine capacity to negotiate. In this manner they obtained the demilitarization of some hospitals, regular crossing of the frontlines and safety arrangements for their movements in the combat zones.

The fact that room for humanitarian action has been maintained in Sri Lanka is due to the importance laid upon democratic values by certain politicians, the government's wish to keep a non-military presence in the areas claimed by the LTTE, the guerrilla's inability to provide some essential services themselves and international pressures.

Sadly, the above trend is contradicted by the systematic and general disrespect of human rights. Humanitarian action soon reaches its limits when terrorism is met with counter-terrorism, when the dividing line between the warring factions is blurred. The activities of militia or units operating in civilian clothes spread insecurity and as massacres are on the increase in the east, humanitarian organizations in the area find themselves coming up against problems which, although not as extensive as those in Peru, are undeniably of the same nature.

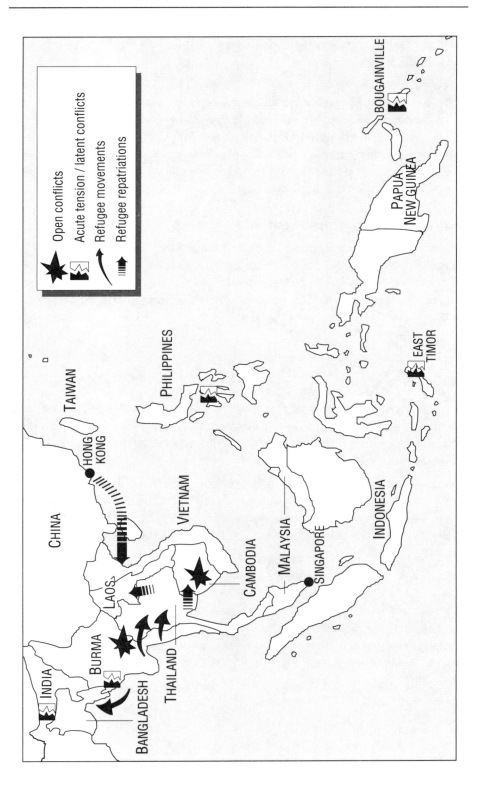

SOUTH-EAST ASIA

Introduction

Troubles never come singly, and the Vietnam war was not followed by any true reconciliation for the Indochinese peninsula. Since 1975, it has lived through a large-scale human disaster. In 1975, the communists replaced the pro-American regimes in Vietnam, Cambodia and Laos, promising a new era of peace and progress. But the winners were heavy-handed in imposing their rule and their economic doctrines were ruinous. In the south of Vietnam and Laos the liberators soon became occupants. Cambodia, left to the fanatical collectivization of the Khmer Rouge soon became a bloodbath. The towns emptied, the borders were closed and the population subjected to forced labour. Stirred up by nationalism, border skirmishes soon degenerated into armed conflicts with the Vietnamese 'comrades'.

The great exodus came as a result of this state of affairs, aggravated by a catastrophic economic situation. From 1976 onwards the Vietnamese started to leave their homeland, first by hundreds, then by hundreds of thousands. First to leave, the people of the south took to the sea in overladen makeshift boats, headed for Thailand, Malaysia, Singapore. On the land side, the Laotians, who only had the Mekong to cross, also arrived in Thailand. The Cambodians however remained prisoners of Pol Pot's henchmen. In 1979, military occupation of Cambodia by the Vietnamese and the armed Chinese reprisal in Vietnam brought new waves of fugitives by sea and land: Hanoi took advantage of this to get rid of its Sino-Vietnamese community and, in Thailand, an estimated 200,000 survivors of the Khmer Rouge's Cambodia suddenly drifted into the border camps.

All the countries in this region were affected by this flight. Dramas and difficulties accumulated, above all in Thailand where the majority of these would-be exiles arrived.

To avoid a tragedy, a challenge of this size needed an exceptional international response. The UN-sponsored assistance operation, in which dozens of governments and hundreds of non-governmental organizations took part was, in some respects, a success. It enabled hundreds of thousands of men, women and children to be saved and assisted. Better still – and this is unprecedented – the movement of sympathy in favour of the Indochinese refugees was translated into a massive policy of open doors, above all in the United States, Australia, France and Canada.

However, this operation was far from faultless. Apart from practical inadequacies, it tolerated political and military interference and violence contrary to humanitarian principles. It did not put an end to the crimes of pirates against the boat people in the Gulf of Thailand. Nor did it stop thousands of Cambodian civilians from being stopped at the Thai border to be used as a supply base and become reserve soldiers and porters for the armed factions, particularly the Khmer Rouge.

Following the Paris agreement on Cambodia (1991) and the setting up of the United Nations plan, the fate of the 380,000 civilians blocked at the border for over 10 years is now on the way to being settled: the repatriation of refugees has started under the aegis of the United Nations High Commissioner for Refugees, although the Khmer Rouge's attitude leaves a lot of uncertainty regarding the future of Cambodia.

Another tragic hangover from these years of exodus, and this is an even greater problem to deal with, 50,000 Vietnamese are parked in detention centres in Hong Kong. There is not much hope for them because generosity is no longer what it used to be. The doors of the Western countries, wide open not so long ago, have closed, and only a few thousand boat people have obtained the status of refugees since June 1988, when this ceased to be an automatic procedure in Hong Kong. The choice for these unfortunate candidates for exile is sadly simple: either they remain in detention or return to Vietnam, by force or of their own free will.

After years of upheavals and tragedies which have thrown millions of people into exile and mobilized international assistance as never before, the Indochinese peninsula, like all of South-East Asia, is gradually returning to a state of peace. The process of returning to normal seems to be well on the way, but it is not devoid of danger as the case of Cambodia illustrates. Nor is it devoid of new crises. In contrast to Indochina, Burma is throwing hundreds of thousands of homeless out on to the roads of exile.

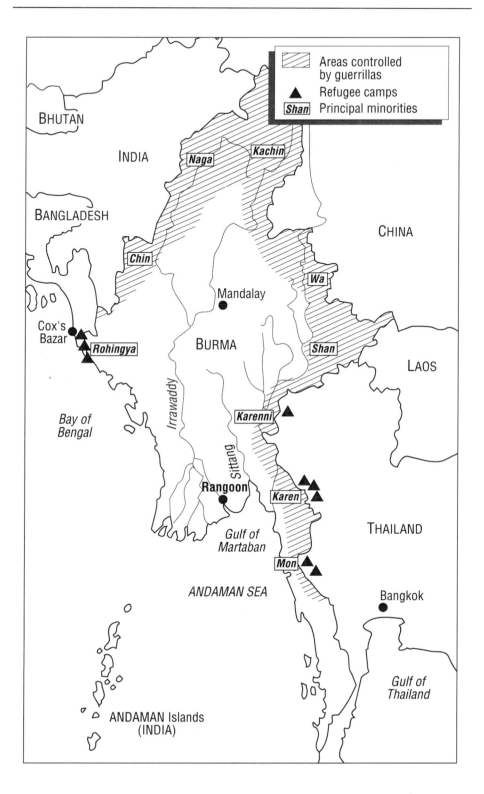

BURMA

For 30 years, Burma has suffered from economic misery and political repression under the iron fist of a hardline military regime. Internal dissent has been smothered at every level of society. This has taken the form of student massacres, the house arrest and isolation of opposition leader Aung San Suu Kyi, the arrest of elected opposition leaders, forced relocation of city dwellers and the persecution of minorities. The product of this overall repression is a flood of refugees spilling over its borders into neighbouring countries. For 10 years, Thailand has been host to tens of thousands of Karen, Mons and Karenni refugees while Bangladesh is once again confronted with a massive exodus of Rohingyas from the western Burmese province of Arakan.

The Rohingya exodus

In summer 1991, members of the Rohingya Moslem minority began to flee into neighbouring Bangladesh to escape increased militarization of Arakan province. At the beginning of 1992, the exodus reached massive proportions: in a few months, more than 300,000 refugees poured across the Naaf border river and sought refuge in a string of camps south of Cox's Bazar. They all tell the same story of intense military activity, destruction of villages, forced labour, pillage, repression and systematic rape of Rohingya women.

The exodus is not unprecedented. Burma, and its Arakan state in particular, suffers periodic bouts of xenophobia. Large numbers of Moslems fled during the Japanese occupation in the 1940s, again in the next decade and in 1978 when the Burmese government unleashed a campaign code-named Naga Min, or Dragon King, which forced more than 200,000 Rohingyas to flee into Bangladesh.

The 1978 exodus came at a time when prices were sky rocketing and public discontent with the country's authoritarian rulers bubbled over. Burma's traditionally militant students launched anti-government protests. The unrest continued for a few years until it was suppressed with military force, resulting in a heavy loss of life. But to distract the population from the country's political and economic difficulties, a campaign was launched against the most vulnerable of Burma's many ethnic minorities, the Rohingya Moslems of Arakan, knowing that this was something of which even the regime's staunchest domestic critics would not disapprove. Anti-Indian sentiments have always been strong in Burma and many Burmese see Rohingyas as simple migrants from overcrowded Bangladesh.

The Rohingyas say that they are indigenous Burmese people who have been living in Arakan for centuries. They stress that migration over the past few decades has gone in the opposite direction: facing discrimination at home, large numbers of Rohingyas have crossed the western border continually since Burma's independence in 1948. The Rohingyas are perhaps the most vulnerable of Burma's numerous ethnic minorities. But they are by no means the only persecuted minority in Burma, nor are they the only ethnic group that has escaped the repression of the military government in Rangoon and sought refuge across the country's frontiers.

In fact Burma has potentially one of the most explosive ethnic compositions of any country in South-East Asia. Sixty per cent of the population are ethnic Burmese, and most of these are Buddhists; they live in the vast central Burmese plain around the rivers Irrawaddy and Sittang. The other 40 per cent belong to an abundance of ethnic minorities – Nagas, Kachins, Chins, Shans, Karennis, Karens, Mons – who inhabit the horse shoe shaped ring of mountains and highlands that surround the central plains.

Thirty years of dictatorship

The first difficult years of independence failed to turn this immense diversity into a functioning, unified country. Army units rose in mutiny, the Karens, the Karennis and the Mons took up arms, and the powerful Communist Party of Burma went underground to organize guerrilla forces. To counter the insurgency, Burma's tiny army – which numbered only a few thousand men at independence in 1948 – was built up to a formidable fighting force of almost 100,000 men by the late 1950s. At that time, the insurgency was more or less under control but the inevitable outcome of the fighting was that the strength of the army grew out of the civilian government's control; it became a state within the state which eventually, on 2 March 1962, seized absolute power.

Coups are hardly novelties in Asian politics, but when the Burmese army, led by general Ne Win, seized power in Burma 30 years ago, it assumed not only political power but also economic control. Purportedly this was done within the framework of a new ideology, 'the Burmese Way to Socialism'. Production, distribution, import and export of all commodities were 'nationalized' – which in effect meant that the army took over

> ## Burmese refugees in Thailand
>
> Since the beginning of the 1980s, military operations against ethnic minorities in eastern Burma have intensified, leading to a continual exodus of refugees towards Thailand. This has successively affected the Karens from 1983 onwards, the Karennis after 1988 and the Mons since the beginning of the 1990s.
>
> Thailand traditionally sees Burma as a potential enemy and has long supported the minority movements which act as a buffer on its border. However, in 1988 Bangkok came closer to Rangoon at a time when the Burmese regime was selling the rights to exploit natural resources such as teak and minerals in rebel territory along the border to influential Thai companies. These minorities lost their Thai support and the Burmese army tightened its hold on the border. Villages, crops and livestock were destroyed and the population was displaced, the adults robbed or subjected to forced labour. This climate of terror triggered the flight of tens of thousands of people who hid far from the villages to escape from the army or sought refuge on the other side of the border. Between 1989 and the beginning of 1992, the number of refugees in Thailand increased from fewer than 20,000 to more than 65,000.
>
> These refugees live in Thailand in precarious conditions, in a region infested with a particularly pernicious form of malaria. Only a few relief agencies are allowed to give them minimal assistance – food and basic medical care. The UN High Commissioner for Refugees is not entitled to intervene and the refugees are given no legal protection. Thus, several dozen Burmese students seeking refuge in Thailand were escorted back to the border in 1989. Since the beginning of 1992, however, a significant increase in the Burmese army's capability seems to have convinced Bangkok that Rangoon should be held at a certain distance but its position remains very ambiguous.

everything from the Burmese business community. Burma's once bustling free-market economy went into a state of decline and the production sector almost collapsed. Burma and its population were soon among the world's poorest.

Given the choice of contraband or no goods at all, which would have resulted in political and social unrest, Ne Win's military government turned a blind eye to smuggling and black market activities along the country's long porous borders with Thailand, China, India and even Bangladesh. By the mid-1980s, the black market supplied Burma with an estimated 80 per cent of all its consumer goods. Ironically, the insurgencies were further fuelled by the 'Burmese Way to Socialism': the Karens and other rebel groups controlled the border areas through which the contraband was smuggled into the country and used the tax they collected on this trade to buy arms, ammunition

The huge exodus of the Rohingyas

Since the beginning of 1992, Bangladesh has faced one of the largest exodus movements in recent refugee history. In a few months, 300,000 Rohingyas have ended up in one of the poorest and most overpopulated countries in the world.

The first camps, hastily set up close to the Burmese border, testify to the immense effort made by Bangladesh to shelter these totally destitute refugees who, at the peak of the exodus, were arriving at a rate of several thousand a day. In less than two months, with the help of the UNHCR and a few relief agencies, the authorities managed to build bamboo shelters for 150,000 people, dig wells and latrines and organize emergency hospitals and nutrition centres for malnourished children.

However, faced with the ever-increasing number of refugees, which reached 300,000 in the spring, anxiety soon replaced this spirit of solidarity. Relief operations met with some difficulty, at a time when overall conditions remained quite poor, particularly in the most recent camps where malnutrition and mortality reached record levels, even when compared to those for Bangladesh which are themselves high.

On 28 April, for fear of seeing the problem become chronic, the Bangladesh government signed a repatriation agreement with the Burmese regime. This agreement aroused anxiety in the camps, where the refugees remember that a shortage of food aid caused their forced repatriation in 1978 after a similar agreement. But in 1992 the Bangladesh government stresses that repatriation should not be considered unless the UNHCR is given the opportunity to monitor security conditions in Burma for the refugees' return. Despite these soothing statements, refugees still fear repatriation.

and other supplies on what is usually euphemistically referred to as the 'Thai black market'.

But the combination of economic misery and political repression inside the country soon became unbearable. In 1988, 26 years of pent-up frustrations with the iron-fisted rule of Ne Win exploded with unprecedented fury, taking everyone, including the Burmese themselves, by surprise. Students, always at the forefront of any political movement in the country's history, took to the streets by the thousands. Their protests were met with unbelievable brutality: police and army units opened fire, killing hundreds of teenagers and young people in their early twenties. But this bloody repression and the subsequent arrest of thousands of students only outraged even more people and led to a widespread protest movement all over the country during summer 1988 which was repressed with bloodshed.

The mass protests in the streets came to an abrupt end on 18 September when the military decided to stage a coup. To placate the restive crowds, and to appease the international community, the new State Law and Order Restoration Council (SLORC) allowed the opposition to set up their own parties and, to the surprise of many, they also promised to hold general elections. These elections, held in May 1990, were a great call for democracy. Despite the fact that its charismatic leader, Aung San Suu Kyi had been placed under house arrest, the National League for Democracy (NLD) secured a landslide victory, capturing 392 out of 485 seats in the assembly. The military chose to ignore the outcome of the election. Instead, dozens of MPs elect and their supporters were arrested. Since then, Burma has been engulfed in overall repression.

Economic and political difficulties inside the country are seen as the main reason why the SLORC decided to target the vulnerable Rohingya minority in Arakan once again. The Rohingyas have always been convenient scapegoats for a regime eager to deflect attention from the economic and political deadlock it created. However, the Rohingyas are not the only victims of this decaying regime, today trying to found its legitimacy on 'Burmese purity': in addition to the 300,000 Rohingyas who have taken refuge in Bangladesh, there are thousands of Karens, Mons and Karennis who, in 1992, joined the tens of thousands of refugees sheltered in precarious conditions by Thailand for the last 10 years or so.

This exodus of refugees from Burma is also partly the result of the events of 1988. In order to remain in power, the SLORC almost immediately embarked on a massive build-up of Burma's armed forces. In 1987, they totalled about 190,000 men. Today, the figure is close to 300,000. This large force has to be kept busy and the outcome is military activity in areas where there is no internal insurgency to speak of, for instance Arakan.

International reaction to the crisis in Burma has so far been ineffective. The Western countries have of course issued numerous statements condemning the repression, but Burma remains one of the most closed countries in the world. Although a few minorities remind us of their existence by crossing over the borders, Burmese society has become more or less mute. Relief organizations cannot help the population inside the country and have to make do with bringing aid to the refugees who have succeeded in fleeing to neighbouring countries. This situation is becoming all the more worrying because of the possible repatriation of Rohingya refugees. In 1978, when the last repatriation was negotiated between the Burmese and Bangladeshi governments, no relief agency was allowed to supervize the conditions of their relocation or to supply protection for them in Arakan. In consequence the violence which had led to their flight resumed again, paving the way for another exodus.

Guerrilla warfare
Political violence
Serious social problems

MEXICO
CUBA
BELIZE
HONDURAS
HAITI
GUATEMALA
NICARAGUA
EL SALVADOR
COSTA RICA
PANAMA
COLOMBIA
VENEZUELA
GUYANA
SURINAME
FRENCH GUYANA
ECUADOR
BRAZIL
PERU
BOLIVIA
PARAGUAY
CHILE
ARGENTINA
URUGUAY

Latin America

Introduction

atin America seems to suffer from a pendulum effect. There has been an apparent return to normality with the peace process currently under way in El Salvador and Nicaragua but the present detente continues to be extremely fragile compared to the all-out violence in most of the countries on the continent.

The swing towards relative peace can be traced back to when Central America ceased being a regional and international conflict zone, on 25 February 1990, when Violetta Chamorro beat the Sandinistas in the Nicaraguan elections. The peace process continued a little later in Salvador after the Farabundo Marti Front for National Liberation (FMLN) and the Cristiani government negotiated a ceasefire and the UN Security Council decided to send 170 observers to monitor the respect of human rights by both parties. Today, for the first time in 20 years, Central America is free from civil wars, despite relentless violence in Guatemala. Furthermore, this same trend towards peace can be seen in other countries on the continent such as Chile and Argentina where key conditions for peace, i.e. the consolidation of democracy and economic recovery, are gradually being achieved.

One should not be misled by this optimistic prospect. The return of peace engenders its own difficulties. In Central America, it means the return of jobless refugees with no land – one quarter of the people of Nicaragua are in this position. It also involves the return to civilian life of tens of thousands of guerrilla fighters or soldiers who for 20 years have known no family other than their assault rifles. This is clearly a hard task, to the point where it constitutes a further challenge for the humanitarian organizations in the region. How can one help these groups which are bound by their former allegiances without locking them up within these allegiances which sprang from a war logic they must now lay aside? Furthermore, arms have not been laid down everywhere: violence and guerrilla warfare is rife in Colombia and Peru against a background of terrorism, army reprisals and drug trafficking.

From a broader perspective, the central American and Andean countries, even Brazil, continue to suffer from their perennial afflictions. The Indians are now in even greater danger of extermination. As in the American Far West, the frontier of – legal or illegal – agriculture moves implacably forward, crushing the Indians in its path. In Guatemala, they have been exterminated, entire communities at a time, for decades on end. In Brazil, they are being chased out of Amazonia by mixed-race small farmers as well as the large food and forestry conglomerates. In Colombia or Peru, it is the drug 'industrialists' who invite the 'civilized' farmers to drive out or kill the Indians to grow coca on their land. In Bolivia, the jobless tin miners also turn to coca growing in order to survive.

The continent as a whole provides a picture of relentless violence: violence between the cities' poor, violence by private armed guards protecting the interests of the rich, violence as a mere instrument in a society riven by political assassination. Even street children turn to crime as their only chance of survival. And violence, above all, is perpetrated against these homeless children, murdered by the police force. In Rio, Bogota, Lima or Mexico City, haphazard urban sprawl has so inflated social exclusion that most people, without proper jobs, live by the black economy or crime.

To end this long list of Latin America's problems, one has to mention the deadly pandemics which are reappearing with a vengeance in the wake of deeper poverty, generalized social distress, the collapse of governments and the spread of shanty towns. Peru especially has consistently accumulated the worst dangers looming on the continent: the horror of the Shining Path's terrorist violence, their collusion with drug traffickers, the massacre of the Indians, the cholera epidemic, the underlying threat of a military dictatorship, the indescribable distress in the shantytowns, to name but a few. Although poverty can be seen all over Latin America, the continent's worst human tragedy today is found in Peru.

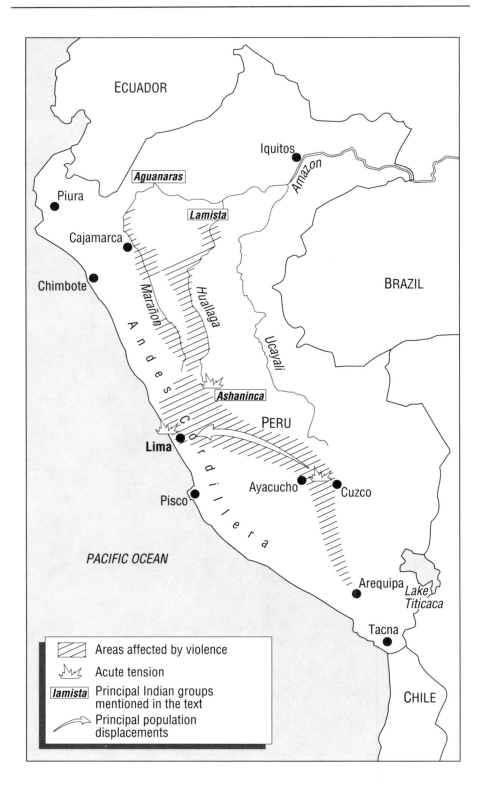

Areas affected by violence

Acute tension

lamista Principal Indian groups mentioned in the text

Principal population displacements

Peru

eru is probably the Latin American country where civilians suffer most. Facing an economic crisis which forces 80 per cent of the working population into the underground economy, they are caught in the crossfire between the various armed factions. These are the Maoist Shining Path guerrillas, joined since 1985 by the Tupac Amaru Revolutionary Movement (MRTA), the police and the army, who treat ordinary citizens hardly better than rebels, the peasant militias, armed by the government since 1990 and, lastly, gangs of killers in the pay of the drug industry. Between 1980 and 1992, clashes between the different groups have caused more than 25,000 deaths, mostly of civilians.

The rural population caught in the crossfire

At the end of the 1970s, a group of Ayacucho University lecturers who were members of the Peruvian Communist Party (PCP) launched the 'revolutionary war' in the Andean areas in the south of Peru. In order to get a foothold in the isolated regions inhabited by Quechua (Ayllu) Indian communities, the Shining Path made subtle use of the Indians' antagonisms and hostility to the central government. This tactic was facilitated by the fact that some of their activists were of Quechua origin. When the Indians attempted to resist the Shining Path, it resorted to extremely brutal methods to hold its ground.

The anti-guerrilla police forces and – after 1982 – the army have proved ill-prepared to face the Shining Path, which simply merges into the population. They use a scorched earth policy and massacre entire villages suspected of sheltering 'terrorists'. In 1984, after the surveillance of such vast areas proved impossible, the army began setting up village self-defence groups. Armed with sticks and catapults, these are easy prey for the guerrillas.

99

Cholera: a worldwide pandemic

Cholera spared the American continent for decades. In January 1991, however, a cholera epidemic broke out in Peru. In a matter of months, the epidemic spread from the coastal towns throughout the entire country, then to Ecuador, Brazil, Colombia, Chile and Argentina. The speed with which it spread in Peru proves how bad the health situation is, more specifically in the shanty towns where one-third of all Peruvians live. Cholera is a poor man's infection, the 'dirty hands disease' which goes with a lack of drinking water. One quarter of Latin America's population has no access to drinking water and one-third has no sanitary means of disposing of excreta. In these countries ill-prepared for the epidemic, information was often handled in an emotional manner, which shows that cholera has an importance which goes way beyond the medical and social cost of the disease.

In Africa, where the present epidemic broke out in 1970, people have learned to recognize cases and handle the problem in a more objective manner. In refugee camps, in particular, which provide fertile ground for flare-ups of epidemics, the steps to be taken are clearly codified. Early detection of cases is followed by treatment of patients in an isolation centre, the disinfection of excreta, decontamination of the sources of infection, etc. While it is difficult to prevent the actual spread of a cholera epidemic particularly in an open urban environment, treating the patients is relatively simple by rehydrating them orally or through intravenous injections to prevent the body from losing all its fluid.

Over 20 years, all African countries have been affected, with a few rare exceptions. Between 1983 and 1989, the World Health Organization registered 65,000 cases in 93 countries, particularly in southern Africa, the Horn of Africa and Asia. By striking Latin America where it is likely to become endemic, the seventh cholera pandemic has now become worldwide. Over 200,000 cases were recorded throughout the world in 1991.

As soon as he came to power in August 1990 – replacing Alan Garcia – Alberto Fujimori decided to gradually arm the 'Rondas de Defensa Civil', the civil defence patrols which in principle came under the control of the army. In actual fact, these often escape all control, as in the tropical areas of the Apurimac region, and commit violence against the local people. As for the army, it carries out reprisals on those communities which refuse to form militias to fight the Shining Path.

Victims of the general violence which has been getting constantly worse since 1980, more than 200,000 inhabitants of the Andean areas of central and southern Peru have taken refuge in the cities, especially Lima. Of these, 100,000 come from the Ayacucho region alone, where they made up 25 per cent of the rural population. These displaced persons have found scarcely better living conditions in the shanty towns, and the poor districts where two-thirds of the capital's seven million inhabitants are already living. For those who are not unemployed, the 30 dollars a month minimum wage scarcely covers a tenth of basic needs. Cholera, which broke out at the beginning of 1991, spread easily in this urban fringe. Above all, taking advantage of this social context and the influx of the Andean peasants, the Shining Path's recruitment drive has been thriving in the shantytowns since 1990, especially among the young unemployed.

The dirty war in Amazonia

Following the failure of the colonization projects launched by the government at the beginning of the 1960s, the rural population of the Huallaga river valley on the eastern flanks of the Andes gradually turned to the growing of coca. The cocaine boom in the United States towards the end of the 1970s caused a 'green gold rush' among Andean people in search of a better life. These migrations were further accentuated in 1982–83 by the century's worst drought on the high plateaux.

As early as 1983, the Shining Path moved into the Huallaga to impose its rule: it wiped out the minor crime gangs, imposed regulations on coca growing, levied taxes on base cocaine exported by air to Colombia. In 1985, the appearance of the MRTA on the Peruvian terrorist scene started off violent clashes between the two guerrilla groups for control of zones of influence and, from 1990, for control of the drug gold-mine.

Specialized police and army units, backed by United States logistics, are fighting both drug trafficking and the guerrillas. In fact, they are often involved in drug trafficking themselves. The drug magnates, who have set up powerful organizations such as the Campanilla Cartel, and their armed groups form alliances with one or other of the existing forces to suit their interests. As on the high plateaux, the local population is taken hostage by the various warlords and it is they who pay the heaviest toll for the conflict. Even worse, the press and humanitarian organizations never hear about massacres of civilians, for they do not have access to these regions.

Indians, who live in the region in relatively large numbers – Aguaranas, belonging to the Jivaro, Lamista, Ashanika and Campa sub-groups – are in danger of falling victim to ethnocide. Not only do the warring factions attempt to enrol them by force, particularly as guides, but some of the natives, such as the Lamistas, also pay a price for the coca boom. They have always grown small crops of coca because they traditionally chew the leaves. To seize Indian land, the drug lords denounce them as illegal producers to draw down repression on them.

Ashanincas

The Indians of the Peruvian Andean foothills have always been known for their fighting qualities. Until the mid-1980s, several groups of Indians beat off all attempts to enter their valley. For this reason, they were given the name 'Kugapacoris', the archers of death. Today, however, the Ashanincas have fallen victim to the rivalry between two particularly violent revolutionary movements.

In 1988, the MRTA, having been expelled from the Huallaga by the Shining Path, undertook the political and economic conquest of the Pichis-Palcazu region, killing several traditional leaders in the process. The Ashanincas of the Pichis and the surrounding area attempted to resist with the very limited means at their disposal.

As for the Shining Path guerrilla group, it tried as early as 1986 to get a foothold in the Ene Valley by starting from Mar province. Three years of fighting with the natives of Cutibireni resulted in the deaths of 400 people on each side and ruined the Campa economy to such an extent that survival became a major problem. Even this did not lead the Shining Path to relent: in 1989, it launched a campaign of forced recruitment aimed at teaching the Indians 'the thinking of Gonzalo', a substitute for the thoughts of Mao. The Ashanincas who resisted were subjected to repeated attacks, when they were not obliged to flee. A number of people who had been enrolled by force in the Shining Path were rescued by the military. Most were suffering from severe malnutrition and associated illnesses such as tuberculosis, acute parasitosis and even cholera. In all, 8000 Ashanincas are thought to have been killed by the Shining Path out of a total population of 70,000.

As if this were not enough, the Ashanincas are in the line of fire of both the drug barons who have designs on their lands and the army's anti-drug champions, not to mention the never-ending advance of the settlers who have no qualms about taking advantage of the general confusion to seize Indian lands.

The worst possible scenario

On 5 April 1992, President Fujimori dissolved parliament and announced a radical constitutional reform and the reorganization of the judiciary. It amounted to reinforcing the power of the army, which already administers half the country. Its units are against all independent popular organizations, and have on several occasions arrested their leaders, as in Cajamarca and Puno, even though they constitute the most effective rampart against the advance of the Shining Path.

The guerrillas have realized this and attack in particular all those who might turn the population away from the 'revolutionary war' such as members of Peruvian or foreign non-governmental organizations, clergymen, leaders of people's organizations and journalists. They do not hesitate to get rid of any person or group standing in their way. Thus two French aid workers and several members of religious orders were murdered in 1991, in some cases after fake trials in which they were accused of 'numbing the people's conscience by giving them food'. Many areas of Peru, in particular the Ayacucho region, have become inaccessible to members of humanitarian organizations and social workers, who see their room for manoeuvre steadily shrinking.

Even in the capital, political leaders are not safe and the people's organizations receive ever more frequent death threats from the Shining Path. On 15 February 1992, Maria Elena Moyano, deputy mayor of the Villa El Salvador shanty town, was assassinated in the street and her body blown up with dynamite. Villa El Salvador is known for the setting up of a self-management system based on grassroots democracy. Sad to say, this further barbarous act of intimidation was effective and those who still dare stand their ground in the face of the Shining Path are few and far between.

For the Shining Path, the time has come for urban guerrilla warfare. Over recent months, it has claimed a growing number of car bomb attacks on civilian and military targets, most of them in the centre of Lima. The rich districts are discovering the violence and fear which up to now were the lot of the shanty town poor. The guerrillas' clear aim is to make the situation as bad as possible in order to render the enemy even more hateful. After it overthrew democracy by forcing Fujimori to confiscate power, the Shining Path is now attempting to destabilize the president to pave the way for military dictatorship. Any attempt at independence in society would then be crushed, leaving the forces of repression and the continent's most radical guerrillas alone, face to face.

PART TWO
Trends

Humanitarian Aid Versus Politics

It no longer makes sense to talk about the international order since the Berlin Wall collapsed, symbolizing the implosion of a world that had become paradoxically both passive and convulsive, or at least unpredictable and irrelevant to any political logic. The self-dissolution of the Soviet Union demolished the bi-polar structure of relations between the superpowers, while at the same time removing the reason for their rivalry. Meanwhile, even though the United States has by no means abandoned its desire for world domination and is even being called upon to expand it – to fill a vacuum as it were – it no longer has the economic resources to follow through, any more than it has an overall stragegy. It should also be borne in mind that the elimination of the landmarks provided by the East/West conflict is not the sole cause of the current worldwide turmoil. Two other, older factors also come into play which have nothing to do with either the demise of communism or the decline of the United States as a major world power.

The first factor, which surfaced along with the Iranian revolution in the late 1970s, illustrates how individual states have been superseded as the only legitimate players on the international stage. This can be taken as read in the case of the European Community, but that is not what we are concerned with here, nor with the de facto sovereignty of the multinationals, or of the IMF and the World Bank. From an overall point of view, from Iran to the Caucasus or to the former Yugoslavia, the by-passing of the individual state is more closely linked to the return of religion as the driving force behind international conflict. It can also be seen in the stream of millions of refugees defying all efforts to monitor or control them and is even more evident in the spread of a more or less legitimate violence which is no longer a state monopoly in the Horn of Africa, Liberia and some countries of South-East Asia, as well as in Peru, Colombia, Lebanon and now Bosnia-Herzegovina.

Not only is the state no longer a significant negotiating partner when it comes to deciding the fate of hostages, the security of development projects or humanitarian work, but the guerrillas with whom it was once necessary to negotiate have also become 'wild cards'. Since losing the somewhat reluctant support of both East and West, they are behaving in a purely predatory manner, with no deeper purpose than day-to-day survival. With the state left on the sidelines, those claiming to take its place have also faded from the scene, shuffling the last cards in the international Great Game.

The world map is again becoming dotted with white spaces that have been rendered inaccessible – in Africa and Burma, Cambodia, Afghanistan, Peru or what used to be Yugoslavia. These regions, which now stand outside the international order, are also those worst affected by the second factor unconnected with the disappearance of East/West landmarks: our own loss of faith in the possibility of real development for a large part of the Third World. The wealthy nations have dropped their pious preaching and are once more beginning to accept the misery of the poor nations as a destiny about which nothing can be done, considering the 'criminality' of those countries' political backgrounds – especially as they feel sufficiently burdened by their East European neighbours.

How should international relations be viewed now?

With all our former certainties turned upside down, what new form of international relations might be considered? For developed countries, the problem obviously lies in shaping policies that are appropriate to the changeability and uncertainty of the current situation. But at the same time, they are also seeking a more gratifying reflection of themselves now that the good guys and the bad guys can no longer be firmly placed in the East and West camps (or vice versa), as they were under the old order. People always like to dress up their actions with good, and if possible humanitarian, reasons.

The second emergence of the United Nations – its true emergence, in fact – appears to be a reaction to this need to fill the void left by the death of old habits. Like a machine with the brake off, the United Nations shook off its paralysis when the leaders of the Eastern and Western blocs, delighted to be no longer enemies, agreed in the Security Council to breathe new life into the organization. That was how the Gulf War came to take place under its wing. Similarly, UN peacekeeping forces or military observers have managed to win back some standing in Cambodia and El Salvador, and later in Croatia and Bosnia. Although UN intervention has proved no more effective than it was in the past, the organization has been given a facelift along with its specialized agencies such as the office of the High Commissioner for Refugees (UNHCR) – and the Blue Helmets are this year's heroes.

However, this new, improved United Nations is only superficial; if we scratch the surface we will find that the ultimate aim of international politics has been turned on its head.

Only a few years ago, the aim of the United Nations – and of most states – was to preserve peace, albeit with overkill capacity, in the European theatre. And, when they were mentioned at all, human rights were used as one more weapon in the super-powers' armoury of arguments, after the Helsinki Agreements. Nowadays the reverse is true. Since there are fortunately no potential enemies at centre stage, the defence of human rights has taken on a leading role as the overt reason for intervention. Peace, on the other hand, is now seen as a mere side-effect of the triumph of human rights, and limited war is now conceivable as a form of 'humanitarian intervention' designed to ensure the survival of a threatened people. The problem is that this generous vision is, like all other policies, subordinate to the national interest. Moreover, it is increasingly tempting to invoke national interest when Western nations, formerly held up to public obloquy by the peoples of the Third World, have acquired a new look, and are now hailed as saviours expected to perform the great redeeming miracle of 'market democracy'.

From state humanitarian aid to the right of intervention

Since French President François Mitterand's visit to Sarajevo, state humanitarian aid and the right to interfere have become synonymous for European governments: one seems to imply the other. For how can we refuse to interfere on behalf of a people in distress, even though their own leaders would rather there were no witnesses so that they might exterminate them at leisure? While it is hard to criticize a policy when it comes cloaked in good intentions, we must nonetheless take care to distinguish between two separate issues.

In fact, private huminatarian organizations such as Médecins Sans Frontières did not wait for the approval of French health and humanitarian aid minister Bernard Kouchner to interfere by providing clandestine aid to people in danger, against the wishes of their rulers. Some were even created for this very purpose, 'interfering' in Afghanistan, Kurdistan and other parts of the world hit by war and oppression. However, they challenged the sovereignty of perfectly legitimate governments because they had a duty to help others which required interference (condemned at the time by the United Nations) while rejecting that other form of intervention: squeaky-clean state humanitarian aid. So much so that MSF and similar organizations grew up not only in reaction to the calculating policies of governments, but also against the 'neutrality' – the law of silence and respect for the authorities – established by the International Committee of the Red Cross (ICRC). These organizations set out to help all victims without asking anyone's permission, while at the same time giving a straightforward account of any human rights violations they observed in the field. This was why MSF recently refused to support an exploratory mission to areas controlled by the Khmer Rouge. Such a mission had no hope of being more than an excursion carefully planned by Cambodian torturers among a silenced people; at the very most it would have led to the sort of sterile conclusions reached by some equally neutral visitors after inspecting the Nazi death camps.

109

There has, however, been a big change since 1990–91, especially when Bernard Kouchner popularized the term 'state humanitarianism' to highlight the amount of resources allocated by France to evacuate citizens of other African countries from Liberia. First of all, he pointed out that the scale of human tragedy often exceeded private organizations' ability to cope in terms of staff, money and materials, but then he endorsed a new view of international intervention by states. Moral justification for the philanthropic diplomacy of the 21st century seemed to have been found.

It was already no secret that humanitarianism was used both as a practical foreign policy tool and to legitimize that policy. And it was infinitely more appealing than military methods, economic pressure, complex negotiations or loans granted to Third World dictators that would never be repaid. The Scandinavian countries and Switzerland, deprived of more traditional ways to make their presence felt, had long been making use of humanitarian aid. The major powers, for their part, noticed that aid handed out by government or inter-government bodies was much more costly and yielded fewer results than that provided by private organizations run chiefly by volunteers. In addition, the volunteers were more highly regarded in the field than well-off state co-operation officials, whereas to the uninitiated they were all the same. This gave national governments, the European Community and UN agencies the idea of subsidising NGOs in this worthwhile and self-interested cause. Although a positive step, this concealed an unpremeditated trap: most of these organizations now depend on public funds or similar sources for more than half their income, rather than on private donors as in the past.

The decisive step was only taken in the past year, when some Brussels officials adopted the proposal for a humanitarian agency to support and provide practical guidance for private NGOs, and when politicians took over the principle of the right of (rich) states to intervene in the affairs of other states for humanitarian reasons. We are currently facing a difficult situation in which we feel we should be pleased that the ICRC is demanding the right to inspect the camps set up in Bosnia by the Serbs, but cannot help noticing – in Yugoslavia or Somalia – that states can use the humanitarian approach as a screen for political inertia while pandering to the altruistic and pacifist feelings of their citizens. Since politics now has a bad press, humanitarianism has come along just in time to woo European voters confused by the Maastricht Treaty. But in the field of human suffering, the problem is that it is used as an alibi for government failure to respond to situations where political intervention is more vital than ever.

The greatest challenge facing NGOs

The borderlines between humanitarianism, emergency mediation and politics in the narrowest sense are still blurred. The distinction is not much sharper between assistance for which people cry out, imposed assistance and the armed protection given to relief workers as a last resort by claiming the right to military intervention. This can hardly fail to remind us of colonial times, when good intentions abounded and gunboats came to the rescue of worthy missionaries beset by natives so lacking in understanding that there seemed little other hope of saving them.

Whether we like it or not, the situations now facing NGOs are just as ambiguous – situations which were not unknown in the past but which are now occurring on a much broader scale. Should we speak out about authenticated atrocities, at the risk of having all humanitarian intervention banned? Should we agree to, or even pay for, international or local armed protection, knowing that it compromises the organizations being protected in the eyes of the warring factions? Should we send medical teams into prison camps where the injured are dying for want of treatment, seemingly becoming the accomplices of the camp guards? Should we step up humanitarian action in general even though this allows politicians to get away with taking no action? Or, on the contrary, should we assert that the answer to human tragedies lies increasingly in political and military intervention, at the risk of turning this argument into an alibi for humanitarian passivity? These are just a few of the issues we should be thinking about now.

The former Yugoslavia is a striking example of these dilemmas. Since it is part of a developed region, it already has highly qualified medical staff and its most pressing need is for drugs and equipment that would seem like luxuries to African or Asian refugees (but should patients undergoing dialysis be left to die?) Meanwhile, Yugoslavia's need for medical supplies is at the mercy of blackmail and manipulation by the various warring factions, not to mention the substantial physical danger to relief workers. Each side regards the aid it receives as a sort of diplomatic recognition, infinitely more valuable than drugs. And every convoy carries a death threat to the people guarding it. What is to be done? Should we concentrate on condemning the hypocrisy of Western policies or continue to intervene on a humanitarian level despite the difficulties, putting up with the compromises involved?

There are no easy answers. All we can be sure of is that the current international situation raises the most difficult ethical and practical problems that humanitarian organizations have ever had to contend with. The time has come for some agonising decisions.

Guy Hermet

NEW CONFLICTS

The location, nature and rules of world conflicts have changed dramatically in the space of three years. This impression that history is speeding up is only partly accurate; it is also linked subjectively to the fact that the conflicts during the previous decade were remarkably stable, even strangely so.

The last major period of rapid change in the world situation was between 1975 and 1980. Far from bringing peace, the end of the Vietnam War in 1975 was followed by an unprecedented spread of trouble spots. The struggle between the United States and the Soviet Union, which for a long time had been restricted to the Indochinese peninsula, began to spread like a cancer throughout the developing world. This happened in southern Africa after Portuguese decolonization in 1974 and the victories of Frelimo in Mozambique and the MPLA in Angola; in the Horn of Africa when Ethiopia fell into Marxist hands in 1977, in the Sahara with tension between Morocco, Algeria and Mauritania over the decolonization of Spanish (Western) Sahara in 1974. It also appeared in Latin America after the fall of Somoza and the arrival in power of the Sandinistas in 1979, as well as the revival of guerrilla movements in El Salvador and Guatemala. Meanwhile, in Asia the Vietnamese 'liberated' Cambodia and the Soviet Army invaded Afghanistan in 1979 and the first fighting took place in 1977 between Tamils backed by India and Sri Lankan authorities enticed by the possibility of an alliance with the United States. And then there was the collapse of several bastions of Western influence: the start of the civil war in Lebanon in 1974, the overthrow of the Shah of Iran in 1979, increased guerrilla activity in the Philippines and fighting between Chad and Libya.

Within five years, the international stage underwent an astonishingly rapid change of scenery. The main point here is that these upheavals soon resulted in lasting stability, although this did not mean peace – never before had the world been the theatre of so many armed conflicts at the same time. Nonetheless they were low-key, seldom moving beyond the stage of guerrilla warfare, and international involvement was carefully kept below the level where there might be direct confrontation between nuclear powers. Non-governmental organizations found that these low-key wars provided the ideal setting for their work. The exploitation of civilians by the warring factions, massive movements of refugees, the major powers keeping their distance, the political inertia of international organizations – all these gave NGOs a dominant and stable role in these conflicts during the 1980s. The events taking place now are overturning this orderly disorder to which we had become accustomed (especially as it kept war away from Europe and provided the NGOs with a cushy job). We must make a distinction between the development of these 'old' conflicts and the appearance of new trouble spots.

The development of old conflicts with a strong East/West connection

The conflicts that started between 1975 and 1980 were generally regarded as peripheral manifestations of the Cold War. Probably too much attention was focused on their external causes: seen in this light, the fighting in Eritrea became a struggle between Ethiopia's totalitarian ambitions and 'resistance' by Eritrean and Tigrean guerrillas. Similarly, the war in Afghanistan was seen as Soviet expansionism versus an 'Afghan nation' that refused to be dominated. The significance of these external factors was overestimated to such an extent compared to local causes that many people felt the mere withdrawal of the major powers would pave the way for peace. They were surprised when, in the early 1990s, this theory turned out to be false. Cuba and the Soviet Union's fast and total pullout from Ethiopia was not enough to settle the problems raised by the long-standing antagonism between Eritreans and what used to be Abyssinia. On the contrary, the Ethiopian empire was more than ever called into question. Similarly, the Soviet withdrawal from Afghanistan did not provide a solution to the country's ethnic rivalries and left intact the 150-year-old problem raised by clashes between local rulers and the modern state trying to govern them.

From Cambodia to Mozambique, from Nicaragua to Sri Lanka, it is quite clear that these conflicts are not due simply to outside influences and cannot be stopped by removing those influences. The growth of violence in these countries is the result of local factors that have changed remarkably little over a long period (ethnic and religious differences, territorial rivalry), and 10 years of fighting has structured their societies around self-perpetuating war economies.

Suddenly the clarion call has changed. Less than five years ago, the major powers were being urged to pull out of these countries; now they are urged not to abandon them. If there is any chance of peace, it will come not as a result of a passive withdrawal on the part of the international community, but from active commitment by those who have so far put all their energy into making matters worse. Moves towards peace in these long-standing conflicts have been much more clear-cut where international action has been most intense. Such action has varied widely according to the countries involved and depends on new interests that have come to the fore. International commitment seems to be taking place on three levels:

Areas of strong involvement. There are some parts of central America and South-East Asia where the major powers, and particularly the United States, are willing to become deeply involved. The support given to the peace process, the major disarmament operations carried out there, the deployment of the United Nations' ONUSAL observer force in El Salvador and UNTAC in Cambodia are evidence of this robust and large-scale involvement.

This does not mean that the future looks bright in these areas. The peace agreements negotiated under the aegis of the United Nations with strong international safeguards are chiefly a diplomatic balancing act which still has to be transformed into genuine political stability. Beneath the blanket of peace the world wishes to throw over them, these societies are still riven by violent antagonisms. The roots of conflict are still intact and there is nothing to suggest that in the long term the social and political forces there will be inclined to rein in their rivalries in the name of peace and parliamentary democracy. In El Salvador, the reunification of the areas held by the FMLN and those held by the government is far from complete, the Khmer Rouge are keeping a firm grip in Cambodia and the resurgence of the Contras in Nicaragua shows that some of its people reject democratic compromise.

Areas of average involvement. In Angola, the agreement between the Soviet Union and United States has produced a ceasefire and the guarantee provided by the United Nations and several other Western countries has played a decisive role in persuading the warring factions to sign a peace agreement providing for free elections. But nothing has been finally settled. The strained stability in the period leading up to the elections has given no indication of how people will react to the results. Tension is still running high, much is at stake in rebuilding the country and all kinds of violence may still occur if there is no lasting international commitment to peace.

In Ethiopia, the United States limited its involvement to supporting the overthrow of the dictator Mengistu Haile Mariam and attempting to stabilize the situation by making it easier for Tigrean guerrillas to take control. Since then, the country has been the scene of ever-increasing chaos. A 'useful Ethiopia' comprising the strategic northern regions of Eritrea and Tigre seems to be moving towards relative stability, while the rest of the country is being torn apart by centrifugal forces aggravated by tension in neighbouring Somalia, Sudan and northern Kenya. There too, Western involvement seems to have stopped halfway and the local roots of conflict are still giving cause for concern.

Areas of low involvement. These include Afghanistan and Mozambique. The way the Afghan conflict developed after the withdrawal of Soviet troops was a result of regional political manoeuvres involving Iran and Pakistan and local military manoeuvres that set the various factions of the resistance and the army against one another. The United Nations kept a low profile and renewed fighting in Kabul led to the evacuation of UN staff and diplomatic representatives.

In Mozambique, which unlike Angola has no oil or mineral wealth to bargain with, peace negotiations are proving extremely difficult. The international community, whose chief concern is to get rid of the burden of two million Mozambican refugees as quickly as possible, is backing the negotiations between the government and Renamo guerrillas, but many governments and international organizations would be willing to accept a signature forced out of the warring factions in order to declare peace in the country and organize the return of the refugees. Unfortunately, the lack of control Renamo seems to have over the armed gangs pillaging the country is a sign that an official agreement would not go far towards bringing real peace to Mozambique.

The way these old conflicts have developed is anything but reassuring. At this juncture the NGOs, and MSF in particular, have a vital part to play that might be described as 'critical help': working alongside the major UN missions, in Cambodia and El Salvador for instance, while standing far enough back to allow them to criticize how these missions are going. Where the return of refugees is concerned – a policy that the financing institutions now regard as a priority – MSF must retain its freedom to evaluate and comment. More than ever, we must ensure that this policy is carried out with respect for humanitarian principles and that people such as the Mozambicans are not compelled to return to their countries if the minimum safety to which they are entitled cannot be guaranteed.

We must continue to keep a close watch on these unstable and potentially volatile areas. Large-scale international operations are expensive and unlikely to last, and we have already seen that they are not enough. Responsibility for maintaining contact with these regions, which are gradually falling into oblivion and plunging into a tragedy made worse by indifference and neglect, will soon be back in the hands of the NGOs.

The new conflicts

The return of wars between states

It is noteworthy that during the 1980s fighting between states practically disappeared, to be replaced by an outburst of internal conflicts. The Israeli-Arab question had, since Camp David, given rise to indirect fighting in the context of the civil war in Lebanon. A few squabbles flared up between African nations but fizzled out just as quickly. The dispute between Chad and Libya, despite or perhaps because of the French intervention, had always been presented as a civil war between Chadians. The only traditional conflict between nations was the long-running Iran-Iraq war – so traditional in fact that it was regarded as a sort of anachronism and dubbed the 'desert First World War'. Obviously the major powers wanted to avoid fighting between states because of the danger that this might develop into a worldwide conflict. The Cold War functioned as a giant insulator, allowing internal instability full rein but keeping conflicts confined within national boundaries.

The current period is characterized not so much by the return of conflicts between states as by the loss of this insulator, which leaves the way open for fighting to become more intense and widespread. The Gulf War was the most spectacular example of an unrestricted international operation, or at least with no other restriction than its political objective. The caution previously imposed by the nuclear threat was cast aside and large-scale intervention by the major powers, especially the United States, became possible. This was what suddenly turned a conflict between states (initially Iraq and Kuwait) into a world-scale problem.

Another aspect of the present situation is the emergence of new states, particularly those that resulted from the break-up of the former Soviet bloc. There are still many quarrels going on within and among them. What would have been considered an internal conflict two years ago (between Armenia and Azerbaijan for example) now falls into the category of a fully-fledged war between sovereign states. Depending on the alliances forged by either side, fighting could now spread to a regional or international arena.

In theory, it is easier for humanitarian organizations to do their work during wars between states than during civil wars. The international rules of war, as laid down in the Geneva Conventions, provide a complete and tested set of legal instruments covering wars between sovereign states. In practice, however, not only are wars between states not conducive to private humanitarian intervention; they make it particularly awkward.

During the Gulf War, the allied command wanted to maintain the fiction of a 'clean war' at all costs, so private humanitarian aid, which carried the danger of the true situation being revealed, was always kept at a distance. Only in Kurdistan was it encouraged – and that was for the equally political reasons of avoiding the destabilization of Turkey by Kurdish refugees, responding to public outrage and bringing the Kurds spectacular support but very little military back-up. To sum up, the Gulf War demonstrated the great extent to which neutral intervention depends on the goodwill of states.

In the restricted fighting between young states, the trend has also been to use all known methods and wage total war with complete disregard for international regulations.

In the guerrilla wars we became accustomed to during the last decade, the weakening of the state often created a 'gap' that humanitarian work could slip through. The new wars between states, on the other hand, often mean the total militarization of society, absolute control of humanitarian aid by the state and the will to use whatever means are necessary to achieve its ends, even if this means deliberately targeting civilians and those trying to help them. This should make us think about the minimum conditions for war legislation; sophisticated laws are apparently pointless if there is not enough international order to enforce them. And if we want new states to comply with this legislation, the older and more powerful nations must set an example when they are engaged in military operations.

The new internal conflicts

From Liberia to the former Yugoslavia, from Nagorno-Karabakh to Somalia, the number of internal conflicts is increasing at an alarming rate. All are the result of many specific factors which are dealt with in detail in the first part of this book. We can, however, make out a number of characteristics that are common to all these fresh outbreaks of violence.

■ *Weaker states*. The weak state has long been known in the Third World. Nonetheless, since the Second World War even the weakest states have somehow managed to maintain their institutions and their borders. Nowadays, in a growing number of cases, even this minimum requirement for survival is no longer possible and we are witnessing the actual collapse of some states. Such crises are provoked by both external and internal factors.

Externally, many weak states suddenly lost their backing with the end of the Cold War. This was the case of former Soviet 'satellites' such as Ethiopia, Angola, Vietnam and Afghanistan which found themselves deprived of 'protection'. In the pro-Western sphere the situation was less dramatic, but many countries were victims of increasing neglect, made worse by the fact that they could no longer put forward the communist threat as a reason for helping them.

Internally, for the past three years we have been witnessing the rapid disintegration of the 'totalitarian cement' that used to hold divided communities together. According to a law described by Tocqueville, it is when constraints are loosened and things are finally improving that explosive tensions are at their height. Revolutions against harsh dictatorships are rare; reforming governments have much more to fear in this respect. The break-up that follows may assume a national or ethnic character. In the case of Yugoslavia, the weakening of federal institutions unleashed claims by the member nations. In many Third World countries the split occurs along ethnic lines, or even clan lines, as in Somalia.

It is worth pointing out that whatever some optimists say, the democratic model is facing just as much of a crisis as authoritarian models. Liberia provided a recent example of the collapse of a well-established democratic consensus, with factions resorting to violence because their rivalries could no longer be kept within the bounds of peaceful institutions. Even transitions to democracy are worrying – especially in west Africa – because the process gives rise to centrifugal, and for the most part ethnic, tensions.

This phenomenon of the weakened state is extremely serious. Those who encourage the process, especially in the name of 'redrawing' borders, should bear this in mind: until now, every time a state has split up the result has been not stability but division into ever-smaller ethnic groups, tribes and other feuding minorities. The so-called prison of peoples has become the last rampart protecting them from all-out war.

Moreover, states which have not yet slipped into anarchy are being driven almost wild with despair at the thought of such a fate. Countries with their backs to the wall have stepped up violence and it is the weakest that are the most brutal. The phenomenon can be observed worldwide – in Burma, Peru, Zaire or Algeria.

■ *The fragmentation of political forces.* Cold-war conflicts were usually between two or three organized camps: the government plus one or two guerrilla movements. Nowadays these forces are becoming increasingly scattered. The tragedy of Somalia described in this book is a good example of the military break-up of conflicts. Armed movements split into rival factions and lose control of their troops, leading to the formation of clusters of rebels without a cause and with no resources, answering to no one and only surviving because of the power a gun gives them.

These circumstances make humanitarian intervention extremely tricky. Contrary to the legend of French doctors tending the wounded with bullets flying round their ears, NGOs have until now only been able to work in war zones under the relative protection of the warring factions. 'Traditional' guerrillas were usually willing to offer such protection because of the international respectability and legitimacy it conferred on them. This is no longer the case in the type of conflict where no one is in control, promises are broken and the best way to get talked about is to kill relief workers rather than protect them.

In addition, a new type of guerrilla movement is growing up in many parts of the world (some have a long history but have been given a new lease of life). Examples include the Shining Path in Peru and the pro-Marxist Kurds in Turkey. Like 'traditional' movements they are highly organized, but there the similarity ends. They reject any references to democracy or human rights and use unrestrained violence, mainly directed at the civilians they claim to be 'liberating'. Humanitarian work is often completely unknown to them. Medical intervention in their conflicts is either impossible, as in Peru, or made difficult by the gulf which separates them from humanitarian principles such as those of MSF, which go beyond simply providing medical care.

■ *The part played by cities.* For 10 years, war was waged in the countryside. The grouping of people in refugee camps led to the development of tried and trusted medical techniques. Now outbreaks of violence occur with increasing frequency in cities, either during conventional wars (as in Yugoslavia) or in guerrilla operations (as in Peru). This is an extremely thorny issue for relief organizations. The interweaving of extreme poverty and war, the number of people involved and access problems have left NGOs floundering. There is every sign that this new trend will continue, raising ever more complex problems in the near future.

Never have there been so many appeals for humanitarian aid. Politicians are increasingly coming to regard it as an appropriate response to wars and fighting. On the other hand, the humanitarian approach has never been so hard or, in many cases, so disappointing, as in the conflicts now emerging. It is always easy to claim to be 'doing something' by sending a planeload of medical supplies or a convoy of food to crisis-hit areas, but a true assessment of their effectiveness, the extent to which we can really improve life for the victims, shows real cause for concern. The chief characteristic of the new order of conflicts is not the geographical spread of unchanging phenomena, but the appearance of radically new problems raising new questions for humanitarian organizations.

Jean-Christophe Rufin

REFUGEES AND DISPLACED PERSONS: A NEW DEAL

In a world turned upside down, refugees are a tragic illustration of the upheavals taking place. They are evidence of the war, famine and oppression that have thrown millions of uprooted people on to the roads of exodus. Even the most isolated countries and the most forgotten conflicts come to the fore of international opinion when refugees begin spilling into other countries. This year hundreds of thousands of Somalis, Sudanese, Burmese Rohingyas and Serbs, Croats and Moslems in Bosnia have been added to the 17 million refugees currently registered worldwide, not to mention the 20 million displaced persons within their own countries.

The developments of these past few months are a sharp denial of the once cherished idea that the end of the Cold War would provide an answer to the haunting refugee question. In 1989 the collapse of the Berlin wall under the weight of asylum-seekers raised hopes of a solution: the end of totalitarian rule seemed to announce that the freedom-hungry Russians, Poles and Romanians would no longer need to knock on Western doors. Likewise the end of East-West antagonism led many to believe that solutions could be found for conflicts that arose from the confrontation of ideologies and that the millions of refugees who had been cowering in camps since the end of the 1970s could finally go home.

For a brief time the very notion of refugee seemed to vanish. Forgetful of the conflicts in the South, Europe suddenly began to worry about its neighbours to the East. As objects of fear, Red Army tanks were quickly replaced by the spectre of a huge migration of the poor, a scare that took on the proportions of a tidal wave by the autumn of 1990. With the media adding fuel to the fire, the dissident had been replaced in the West's imagination by the migrant, and the freedom to travel, so long demanded by Western democracies, was sacrificed to fear of an invasion.

It did not take very long for the European countries to be brought back to tragic reality, i.e. that of the massive flights caused by war and insecurity. Somalia, Burma and, above all, the former Yugoslavia have reminded public opinion that behind the bad dream of a Europe submerged by a flood of immigrants, real tragedies have been enacted against a background of a rise in minority interests, exacerbation of old antagonisms and an explosion of nationalism.

Through their violence and their upheavals, these identity-based rifts demonstrate a two-fold breakdown: the first order, forcibly imposed, of communism in the East, and the second one, aborted as it was coming to life, of the 'New World Order'. The number of asylum-seekers continues to grow and conflicts are multiplying. The refugee question is back on the agenda, next to immigration, and it poses a direct challenge to European refugee policies and raises new questions about international instruments of protection.

From refugees to immigrants

The refugee question has evolved because of the disintegration of the Eastern bloc and the splintering of the Soviet Union. It would have been astonishing if this global phenomenon, at the confluence of border, conflict and migration problems, were not affected by the resurgence of nations, the stirring of minorities and the failure of economies. But as the end of the Cold War ushered in profound upheavals in Europe, it also brought about a change in the way refugees are considered.

The story of the boat people was a significant example of this evolution. The Western world was deeply moved by this tragedy at the end of the 1970s: the belated discovery of the human consequences of the communist victories in Vietnam and Cambodia accelerated both the decline of political idealism and the rise of the humanitarian movement. At the same time the tragedy took on an unusually broad dimension because of unprecedented media coverage and, in the United States, the bitter memory of the Vietnam war. Seen on every television screen in the world, the boat people become symbolic victims. They were victims of war, of totalitarian rule, of pirates and the China sea. Outraged Western countries reacted in an unprecedented fashion: for a while the refugees acquired a positive connotation and were welcomed with open arms – but then what defines a refugee is not only persecution but also the feeling of a special responsibility for their fate.

Since then, the Cold War has vanished, the 'Vietnamese syndrome' has faded away, and compassion has grown weary. The boat people have lost their political heft, their symbolic status and their media visibility. They are now treated on the same footing as the Albanian boat people, who were sent back to poverty by the Italian authorities, or the Haitians returned to dictatorship by the American Coast Guard in total disregard of the principles set out in the 1951 Convention on Refugees. The major difference is that the Vietnamese are not pushed back to sea and still have the right to ask for asylum. But since the South-East Asian countries introduced a screening procedure, few of the boat people have been granted refugee status. Most of them are considered illegal immigrants and have no other choice than indefinite detention or repatriation – either voluntarily or under coercion – to Vietnam.

Once recognized a priori as refugees, boat people are now seen as potential economic immigrants. This change of climate, which is especially obvious in the case of the boat people, can be seen just about everywhere in the world, except, perhaps, in Africa and the Middle East. But the Kurdish crisis demonstrated the international community's concern to avoid any new refugee problem, even if it meant protecting the repatriated Kurds in their own country, however temporarily. At other times these uprooted people would have been hailed as 'freedom fighters' and the international community would have been keen to find them a refuge. Nowadays the international community seeks only to avoid any destabilization and to shrug off the 'refugee burden'. Cold War certainties have given way to deep concern for the world's upheavals and fear of migrations. The time is past when refugees testified to the superiority of democratic systems and the 'great misery' of communism. Refugees are now seen as undesirable in countries that have turned in on themselves and are haunted by the idea of invasion. Refugees no longer 'vote with their feet'. The European countries no longer see the problem with a benevolent eye. They now look to reduce the problem by encouraging refugees to return home and by dissuading asylum-seekers from knocking at their doors. Once placed under the heading of human rights, the refugee question is now put in terms of repatriation in the Third World and of control over flows in industrialized countries.

The rise in the number of asylum-seekers in Europe has speeded up this change in policy. Europe has been faced with an increasing flow of asylum-seekers since the mid-1980s. But the asylum problem in the developed countries – essential as it may be as a founding principle of the Western democracies and as the main factor in European integration – remains a marginal aspect of the refugee question. First of all because, with some exceptions, relocation in Western countries is not a suitable solution. Secondly, despite their growing numbers, asylum-seekers still represent only a small part of the world's recorded 17 million refugees. The crucial question of asylum in Europe must not make us forget the massive phenomenon of war refugees. long overshadowed by the glamourous figure of the dissident and today rejected for fear of the immigrant.

War refugees

Most of today's refugees are running away from war and insecurity. In contrast to asylum-seekers who come one by one to the doors of European countries, war refugees travel en masse to neighbouring regions and countries. Mass flights took place during the wars of decolonization but they only became visible to the Western public at the end of the 1970s. At that time the intensification of East–West tension and the increase of 'peripheral' conflicts caused massive exoduses. In Afghanistan, Central America, South-East Asia and the Horn of Africa, millions of refugees provided evidence of the brutality of war and the distress of civilian populations. Third World refugees became a central item on the international agenda. The UNHCR saw its resources rise, and Western governments increased their initiatives in the camps set up on the borders of countries at war. But year after year exile became permanent in these 'humanitarian sanctuaries', which contributed to perpetuating conflicts. Guerrilla movements found political legitimacy through their control over refugees, economic support in the aid poured into the camps and a reserve of potential fighters. Though hostages of the guerrilla movements, the refugees at least received aid and international protection in the camps, which was cruelly lacking for the populations displaced inside their national borders and who were subjected to the pressures and exactions imposed by armed factions.

With the end of the Cold War it was hoped that things would calm down and allow refugee populations and displaced persons to return safely to their home areas. And in a few cases this new climate did allow the international community to contribute to finding political solutions, even if the final outcome is still in doubt. Hundreds of thousands of refugees in Namibia, El Salvador and Cambodia have thus been repatriated – or will be soon – under the aegis of the UNHCR. But most conflicts remain unresolved, condemning millions of refugees to further miserable exile. And new wars are breaking out, causing hundreds of thousands of new refugees and displaced persons to flee to safety.

Improvement in the international situation has not been enough to defuse certain conflicts that were kept going for so long by the superpower rivalry and which are now continuing under their own steam. Mozambique and Afghanistan are two singular illustrations of these conflicts that began in the shadow of the Cold War but have now taken on their own autonomy to more or less international indifference. The withdrawal of the Red Army from Afghanistan has not brought about peace. The Manichaean and orderly struggle of the Jihad against the occupying Soviet troops has given way to a more fluid and volatile configuration with the different ethnic and religious segments of Afghan society pitted against one another. But just as ideological interpretation of the conflicts obscurred the importance of local factors for so long, the much-favoured ethnic approach today must not make us forget the upheavals caused by war.

Afghanistan has been dismantled by 13 years of war. Half the population have left their villages, more than a third have sought refuge in neighbouring countries, and an entire generation has grown up in camps. Time will be needed for Afghan society to rebuild itself in the turmoil of central Asia. In Mozambique too, displacements of population are also a key element of the war. The whole country has become a vast no-man's-land in which the people – kidnapped by Renamo, relocated by Frelimo or fleeing the country – are being pushed around as pawns in a conflict that has no other justification than the interests of armed gangs. Even though some of the political, ideological and ethnic antagonisms that initially triggered them have died down, these conflicts have become the norm and feed on themselves. On the ruins of the state and in the absence of a referee such conflicts have been privatized, armed factions have turned to crime and created a predatory economy based on plundering and trafficking of all sorts. This development has nowhere been faster or more radical than in Somalia, where the civilian population is desperately trying to keep out of the way of pick-up trucks loaded with machine-guns weaving a web of terrible famine. No one can say what actually remains of Somalia in the throes of insecurity that is spreading to the entire Horn of Africa. Borders themselves are disappearing and with them the theoretical distinctions between refugees and displaced and repatriated persons, who are wandering between war and famine in search of minimum food and safety. In Sudan however, the distinction between refugees and displaced persons is easy to make. The former have managed to reach Kenya and Uganda, where they are being helped by the international community. The latter are more than ever inaccessible in southern Sudan. The situation is all the more serious for, having neutralized humanitarian organizations, the Islamic regime in Khartoum has begun a vast project of forcibly relocating whole populations, in order to transform the country's ethnic and religious balance. Of all these seemingly endless wars, the one in Sudan is probably the cruellest. Its displaced populations are the first to be caught in the grip that is slowly tightening around the southern part of the country.

As if these wars were not enough, new conflicts keep appearing that result in the same massive flows of refugees and displaced persons. In Sri Lanka, the Caucasus and especially in the former Yugoslavia, population displacement is not only the consequence of war but the reason for it. While controlling populations is the basic aim in most internal conflicts, the goals of these new wars are the control of territory through forced displacement of populations. Massacres of civilians, on the increase in the eastern part of Sri Lanka, are also part of a strategy aimed at exacerbating tension between communities in order to change the ethnic balances to the advantage of some. In Nagorno-Karabakh too the two sides have each undertaken to occupy or empty parts of the enclave in order to create a fait accompli or reinforce 'historic rights'. But nowhere more than in Bosnia has war been dominated by such an obsession with territory and 'ethnic purity'. The conflict may be summed up as a policy of terror to get rid of the 'undesirables' in order to 'cleanse' the mixed regions and maintain control over 'ethnically pure' areas. The Serbs are being driven by an implacable determination in this frightening massacre; the Moslems are being forced on to the roads, and humanitarian organizations, at the risk of seeming to approve this forced population transfer, are limited to helping them. Now paying the price for not assuming its political responsibilities at the beginning of the Yugoslav conflict, the international community has put itself in a position of helping the odious process through humanitarian aid even if it means discarding its obligations on the issue of asylum on the pretext of not wanting to encourage 'ethnic purification''. The former Yugoslavia throws a particularly harsh light on the failure of the European countries and constitutes the moment of truth for policy towards refugees, for it is on Europe's very doorstep that these victims of war are now gathering.

Protecting the people uprooted by war

For the first time since World War II, Europe is faced directly with a massive exodus of refugees. The problem of war refugees, which had hitherto seemed confined to Third World countries, is once again haunting European countries, raising new questions on the international mechanisms of protection that were brought in 40 years ago. The present system was put in place in 1951 with the signing of the Convention on Refugees and the creation of the UNHCR. Most of the 30 million people displaced by the war were then reinstalled while Europe settled durably into the Cold War and refugees took on the profile of dissidents.

Despite its global appearance, the 1951 Convention only applied to Europe. It was not until 1967 that the UNHCR's mandate was extended to the entire world and that the reality of refugees in the Third World – soon to account for the largest part of the world's total number of refugees – was taken into account. But as the 1951 Convention was based on individual persecution, it proved to be especially out of tune with the refugee question, most of them fleeing conflicts and turmoil collectively. The United Nations General Assembly extended the UNHCR's de facto field of activity to allow it to confront the massive flights caused by war and insecurity. But, although the definition of the refugee has been widened from persecuted individuals to mere victims it continues to ignore displaced persons who, like refugees, are trying to get away from war but without crossing national boundaries. By remaining in their own countries they receive no protection. It has long been true that displaced populations are therefore subjected to violence amid general indifference. International humanitarian law, however, makes no distinction between refugees and displaced persons. Article 3 of the Geneva Conventions and the 1977 protocol dealing with non-international armed conflicts establish the principle of protecting all victims of conflicts, especially displaced populations.

The Yugoslav conflict powerfully brings home the tragedy of populations uprooted by war and their need for protection. Faced with the biggest exodus of refugees in Europe since World War II, European governments cannot limit their help to humanitarian aid and duck their political responsibilities indefinitely. It is their duty to respect the obligations they agreed to in the 1951 Convention and to reassert – and have respected – the basic principles of international humanitarian law. The first obligation of states is to honour the right of asylum. The second is to implement swift and fair screening procedures: in an uneasy atmosphere of xenophobia, restrictive immigration policies and increased population movements, criteria must be found for protecting the most vulnerable. The third obligation is to protect people uprooted by war. But protecting war refugees does not necessarily end with their resettlement in a third country: they must also be assisted and protected from the exactions that forced them into flight in the first place. Confronted with the Yugoslav tragedy and many other bloody conflicts, the international community has an essential role to play in preventing displaced populations from being abandoned to violence and arbitrary action.

François Jean

Refugees: in need of a definition or of protection?

Refugees lives are made more uncertain by the vagueness of their legal definition. There are two views on how they should be protected, which lead to two definitions of refugee status.

When the UNHCR was created in 1951, it came up against the following paradox: to protect someone, one needs to define them, and defining them implies excluding them.

According to the 1951 Convention, a refugee is a person who 'owing to well-founded fear of being persecuted for reasons of race, religion, nationality, membership of a particular social group or political opinion, is outside the country of his nationality and is unable or, owing to such fear, is unwilling to avail himself of the protection of that country'.

The protection given to refugees lies in granting them a legal status and rights similar to those enjoyed by the citizens of a host country.

The United Nations extended the mandate of the HCR on several occasions to deal with massive flows of refugees fleeing war or famine, not from personal persecution. At a time of exodus, the need to confront an exceptional situation and to take concrete action by providing vital services such as security, food and medical care, matters more than the idea of qualifying refugees one by one.

This is the reason why humanitarian law contained in the 1949 Geneva Conventions and the 1977 Additional Protocols does not give a definition for refugees. It only mentions persons who do not enjoy the protection of any government. Humanitarian law does not set out to grant them the same rights as nationals, but it ensures that they are given humane treatment.

Threatened with famine, hostility and lack of recognition, refugees are paradoxically granted more and more assistance. Often unrelated to law altogether, assistance is increasingly precarious, if not insufficient to ensure their dignity and survival. Instead of questioning our own sense of humanity, we continue to get bogged down in the maze of definitions, thus casting doubt on the very nature of refugees.

Françoise Bouchet-Saulnier

Why Famine?

For a good number of Europeans, Africa remains above all the continent of epidemics and famine. The pictures of the skin-and-bone bodies of Biafra and Ethiopia remain etched in our memories. But great famines are not, fortunately enough, the common fate of African countries; they are still exceptional events, clearly limited in space and time.

In 1985 individual donors and governments were generous in their response to the dramatic events in Ethiopia. Famine is back seven years later, on an even greater scale and more deadly than in Ethiopia, yet it has been ignored for too long and is happening amid almost total indifference.

Famine-malnutrition-drought

Famine is still too often confused with chronic malnutrition. The latter is caused by a food imbalance affecting the most vulnerable social groups and resulting in retarded growth among children. The problem, which affects millions of people throughout the world, cannot be remedied without appropriate measures of economic and social development. Over the last 40 years a large number of countries have managed to reduce this phenomenon, but in some cases it is getting worse.

Famine is defined by a sudden reduction of available food for an entire population followed by a sudden increase in mortality. In individual terms this means acute malnutrition that is seen in severe weight loss through muscle wasting – marasmus – or by the appearance of generalized oedemas – kwashiorkor. These two acute malnutrition syndromes are accompanied by deficiencies of vitamins and trace elements and make children very vulnerable to respiratory infections, diarrhoea-related diseases and skin diseases. Mortality rates in such instances are very high, especially among children. Famine calls for emergency measures, especially therapeutic care in medical feeding centres.

There is a second misconception concerning drought and famine. Climatic conditions are only one factor that can lead to famine. Absence of rain only becomes a human disaster if the population cannot be helped in time. Whereas most droughts never become famines, they cause the publication of erroneous figures of 'starving people' supplied by aid-hungry governments. Data from some international sources, such as the FAO and the World Bank, that compile such figures are printed everywhere in the world. According to the best sources, one could read that this year, 40, 60, even as many as 115 million people were 'affected by famine'. The release of such figures is not only meaningless, it also brings about 'donor fatigue', public fatalism and indifference.

The use of 'governmental sources' sometimes borders on the absurd. Somalia, for example, in 1991, deep into civil war, no longer declared anything at all and was therefore sometimes left off the list of countries in danger. Likewise, last year the United Nations announced a terrible famine that never happened, perhaps in part thanks to the appeal it sent out. But when famine really hits as in 1992, public opinion is understandably confused and barely reacts. A sharp perception of the phenomenon was further complicated this past winter when the term 'famine' was improperly used to describe food shortages in the former Soviet Union.

The 1992 drought

It is entirely true that for the past 10 years southern Africa has been struck by a dramatic, unprecedented drought. Grain production of 11 of the region's countries stands at half the normal level, and in South Africa it is only a third. Food imports, according to always questionable estimates, should be as much as 10 million tons in 1992 compared to two million normally. Nowadays high-tech systems, using satellite observation and land-based assessments – state of harvests, prices in country markets, etc. – forewarn of the consequences of a drought so that food supplies can be imported to fill the gaps in deficient areas. This year Botswana, South Africa and Namibia were able to react in time. Zimbabwe, short of foreign currency and in the midst of economic reform, continued exporting grain although negative warning clouds kept gathering. The country is now having a hard time but the good state of its infrastucture has so far helped to avoid the worst. In Mozambique things are going dramatically wrong because of the war and the lack of usable roads. Some regions, notably the north, are producing an excess, but there is no way to transport the grain to the regions that need it.

At the beginning of 1992 rainfall in the Horn of Africa was only a quarter of the average, but it was the war and unsafe conditions that pitched millions of people into famine. The drought only aggravated the situation.

The famine areas

The populations affected by famine are for the most part found in five countries: Mozambique (central and south), Somalia (except Somaliland), Ethiopia (south and east), Sudan (south and west) and Kenya (east). There are pockets of famine elsewhere

130

(Liberia, Sahel) but they are not on the same scale. It is estimated – always a difficult job in the absence of reliable statistics – that in August 1992 more than six million people were actually starving, with no food at all, and that an equivalent number would be under threat very shortly if food aid did not reach them. In the other countries affected by drought, the usual commercial imports should in theory be enough to keep the spectre of famine at bay.

The great famines of the 20th century have been caused by deliberate strategies (the Ukraine in 1921 and 1928, China from 1958 to 1961), serious drought and inadequate aid (Bengal in 1943, the Sahel in 1973), conflicts (Biafra in 1968) and often a combination of these factors (Sudan in 1988 and Ethiopia in 1985). In 1992 famines are still caused by varying factors, but it is possible to highlight the precedence of one or another.

Famine through indifference

In 1985 Kenya was hit by drought and food shortages just as serious as in neighbouring Ethiopia, but the problem was brought under control. Supplies were imported and distributed through normal channels and there was no famine. This 'non-event' went largely unnoticed at the very moment that Ethiopia was sinking into an unprecedented disaster.

Seven years on, eastern Kenya is again afflicted by drought but this time famine was not predicted in time. Miscalculations by the ethnic Somali herders living in the region, Kenya's economic slump and political uncertainty, its lack of reaction to warnings from local authorities, the priorities granted to the people of Nairobi and the ethnic groups with more political clout, and lastly, tardy official recognition of both the famine and the appeals for international relief: all go to explain why Kenya this year has not reacted to the danger as it did in 1984.

Famine as a result of conflict

A typical example is that of Somalia, but eastern Ethiopia, central and southern Mozambique and southern Sudan are also affected to a slightly lesser extent. What happens first is that crops and cattle are destroyed, business networks fall apart and production is put on hold. The economy is thereby weakened, and society disintegrates. Farmers, who are largely self-sufficient, can no longer produce and are forced to join the crowds of refugees and displaced persons in search of food. Next, the war gets in the way of aid operations and prevents relief agencies from reaching the starving. Famine triggers even more violence as paltry food reserves and international aid stocks are fought over. The vicious circle closes on itself.

Against this background of war and aid problems, the warring factions try to interfere with relief operations in order to control the population, especially by the forced relocation of large groups of people. A new food shortage follows. Unlike refugees, who can generally obtain minimal help in neighbouring countries (Kenya or Malawi), displaced persons are often caught in a tragic trap. Uprooted and disorganized, they can no longer rely on local solidarity and find themselves at the mercy of armed gangs. In Somalia and Mozambique nearly half the population has been displaced by war and famine. The people of Mozambique are pawns in the conflict. The Renamo rebel group holds starving people in its grasp and prevents them from reaching refugee camps or government-held zones. The government forcibly groups together the displaced people it has 'recaptured' from Renamo, although it does not have the means – or the will – to feed them. In both Mozambique and Somalia, one can find food-rich areas with pockets of displaced, starving people blending in with more or less correctly fed locals. Finding, having access to and helping these people becomes even more difficult. Violence, shortages, displacements, insecurity and inaccessibility to aid reinforce one another and aggravate the famine.

Orchestrated famine

The Sudanese government is carrying out a vast political project of restructuring society which aims to shake up the country's demographic, ethnic and regional balances. It deliberately uses food aid, even famine if necessary, to do so. In 1988 it prevented international aid from reaching victims of the war. More than 250,000 people died of hunger amid general indifference. In 1992 humanitarian organizations and reporters were still barred from most of the regions of this huge country – five times the size of France. A shroud of silence is gradually descending over Sudan. The food situation in the south is thought to be catastrophic. Hundreds of thousands of people, most of them Christian refugees from the south, have been chased out of Khartoum and sent into the desert where they are totally at the mercy of Islamic organizations and the government for their survival. It should be noted that Sudan had an excellent harvest in 1991 and continues to export grain. If famine continues to spread, it will be the result of a political project, the determination to reshape the country by wiping out an entire section of its population.

Aid and the international response

Once a drought is located, governments, the World Food Programme (WFP) and the main donor countries – if they are willing – organize food imports that serve in most cases to counter famine. This year the United States and the EEC – through the Special Plan for Africa – have voted emergency programmes. Inevitably, however, there is a certain inertia. Given the exceptional requirements in 1992, supplies have not always been sufficient, and grain often arrived too late. The food 'pipeline' remained almost empty for several weeks in the Horn of Africa.

And the relief aid still has to get to the victims. We know that a country is rarely totally affected. Famine relief should come up against serious obstacles only in the regions affected by war. But even in relatively 'simple' cases such as Kenya's, aid is often slowed by red tape or problems with customs.

In Sudan, the fight against famine requires political pressure. But what can be done when the government remains indifferent? Helped by Iran and Iraq, Sudan is already excluded by most cooperation agreements and the Lomé conventions. However, the government keeps using its starving people to blackmail others for aid.

A slightly academic debate took place in the middle of the Somali tragedy. There were those who favoured a political solution and an initial deployment of UN troops before the international community launched any large-scale relief operation. Then there were those mostly private organizations who favoured an immediate operation to 'flood' the country with food in order to diminish the violence linked to the shortage. The International Committee of the Red Cross chose to mount a countrywide operation while the UN – absent for an entire year – waffled and demonstrated its incapacity to respond to the situation, despite the personal efforts of Mr Boutros Boutros-Ghali. The UN and its specialized agencies – UNICEF and the WFP – once again weighed in with too little too late. For months on end a few private organizations – ICRC, MSF, SCF – provided the only aid and the only link with the outside world. It was not until August 1992 that relatively large-scale international aid was sent to Somalia.

Neither inevitable nor surprising

Famine does not just happen by chance. Neither inevitable nor a surprise, it is the result of indifference, a conflict or political calculations. Governments can often intervene to stop a situation from suddenly worsening. India, for example, is regularly struck by drought (1963, 1977, and the most serious one, in 1987) but it has an effective system for monitoring climatic change. There has not been a famine in India since 1943.

The limited phenomenon of famine cannot spread to an entire continent. It can be successfully fought if the various issues at stake – malnutrition, drought and famine itself – do not get confused and are appropriately confronted one by one. This often means combining humanitarian action with media awareness and political pressure on national governments and donors.

Concern remains that the spread of ethnic conflicts and the turmoil now affecting large sections of Africa will only complicate the delivery of food aid. The Somali and Liberian precedents, where society simply disintegrated, can hardly be seen as encouraging.

Alain Destexhe

EPIDEMICS IN THE WAKE OF CONFLICT

In those countries generally classified as 'Third World', civil war or confrontations between ethnic groups or clans are always accompanied by violence, exactions and population displacement. The turmoil not only takes its toll of immediate victims but also – and this can be seen in every case – has dramatic consequences, in the longer term, for groups and individuals, a main one being epidemics.

The countries mentioned in this book are unequally endowed in the health field. Their medical facilities are fragile, insufficiently equipped, badly funded, often serviced by personnel of doubtful competence who are generally poorly paid and, as a consequence, not very motivated. Even when they function only with difficulty, these health systems can keep the traditional endemic scourges at bay. In an armed conflict, independent of the length or intensity of the fighting, the health of the people concerned will be profoundly affected. The health infrastructure, already uncertain, quickly becomes inefficient due to transport problems, maintenance and fuel problems, lack of medical reserves and difficulties in restocking, and, of course, the flight of civil servants and health personnel.

In any given region, the reappearance and sudden flare-up of an endemic disease are related to a stream of upsets provoked by the conflict. War often has one of the following three consequences – or all three simultaneously: 1. It provokes movements of population, which can introduce a new illness into the host population, or expose a weakened population to an illness from which they had previously been spared. 2. It hinders opportunities to control and eradicate vectors of the illness. 3. Through the absence of detection and treatment, it increases the number of cases of the illness so that it reaches epidemic proportions.

Sleeping sickness, malaria, cholera

In Uganda, the region of Moyo in the north of the country has been profoundly affected by clashes between the army and guerrillas. Before the turmoil began, trypanosomiasis

– or sleeping sickness – was endemic and kept 'under control' both by treating the people affected and fighting the tsetse fly, which carries the disease. When Idi Amin Dada was overthrown at the end of the 1970s, most of his ethnic group fled to neighbouring Zaire or southern Sudan to escape reprisals by the Acholi, the ethnic group of his successor, President Obote. Following these events, the whole region of the western Nile was devastated and deserted. Fields reverted to bush and, of course, all health activities came to a standstill.

As the situation improved a few years later, the exiled populations returned home, thanks to a UNHCR repatriation programme, and progressively settled down on their former lands. Relief organizations rehabilitated health facilities and relaunched medical activities. During their exile, a certain number of those repatriated had contracted sleeping sickness in southern Sudan; others returned to areas infected by the tsetse fly, which had proliferated in the meantime in the absence of any control programme.

As a result, a real epidemic of sleeping sickness – always lethal if not treated – broke out in the region. Almost instantly, dozens of cases began to show up at the dispensaries and hospitals, often in an advanced and incurable stage of the illness.

A return to acceptable levels of security allowed the launch of a programme for detection, treatment and prevention on a large scale: since 1987, more than 5000 cases have been successfully treated and a programme to eradicate the tsetse fly has again been started in the area. However, no action against the seat of the infection in southern Sudan has been possible up to now.

In Ethiopia, in 1985, tens of thousands of refugees fleeing the cumulative effects of the drought and the war between the Wollo army of Addis Ababa and the Tigrean guerrillas came together in an immense congregation of people at Korem.

On this high semi-desert, wind-swept plateau conditions of survival were appalling and water was rare. The few aid agencies which attempted to feed the refugees found themselves facing immense operational difficulties. Food was difficult to get to the refugees, the tortuous geography combining with the effects of the war to slow down aid operations.

Cholera had never really affected these high areas. It lived in fragile balance in the plains and showed up from time to time in the form of small, and self-limiting, outbreaks. Travelling with the refugees, it made a sensational arrival in the Korem camp: hundreds of cases suddenly appeared among this weakened population, killing 20 per cent of those affected. Later on, epidemics of typhoid, measles and recurring fevers hit the camp.

Security problems usually aggravate such situations by hindering access to health facilities. This fact is illustrated by the kala-azar epidemic – a lethal form of tropical parasitosis – which has been rampant in the western region of the Upper Nile and southern Sudan since 1988. Population movements produced by the war which ravaged this area have probably determined the outbreak of the disease in a population previously unaffected. The extent of the epidemic, which has probably claimed tens of thousands of lives, can also be explained by the isolation of the area and the almost total destruction of its health infrastructure.

At the cost of considerable risks incurred by the medical teams and with the help of versatile logistics, health centres have been set up allowing the treatment of a thousand patients at a time in extremely difficult conditions. There is no doubt that many other sick people are unable to reach the centres – and are out of reach of any therapeutic help.

In Cambodia, malaria probably killed tens of thousands of people when a large part of the population, principally town-dwellers who had never been exposed to the parasite, were deported en masse by the Khmer Rouge to the ricefields and forests as forced labour. Some years later, the Khmer Rouge were pushed back to the borders by the Vietnamese army. Once again, tens of thousands of people were conscripted by force by the new regime for the construction of strategic defences along the Thai border. In these forest zones, infested with multi-resistant strains of malaria, a new epidemic wiped out thousands of these 'voluntary' workers. Still today, hundreds of thousands of Cambodians in the countryside remain at risk of malaria with virtually no means of appropriate treatment. After 20 years of war, Cambodia will require an enormous amount of aid to face this situation.

These examples show the direct impact of conflicts on the emergence of epidemics and on the usual means of confronting them. In countries with fragile health structures, a return to normality – either peace or, at least, conditions allowing health measures to be taken – does not have an immediate effect on health: it often takes years, if not decades, to see a return to the original conditions.

Philippe Biberson

CRISIS MEDICINE

An immediate and efficient response to the misery of displaced or refugee populations, whether victims of conflict or of natural disaster, depends not only on the work of medical teams in the field, but also on the deployment of overall assistance covering basic needs (water, food, shelter, etc). This response, if it arrives early enough, will ensure the survival of the greatest number, but the experience of the past 20 years shows that it depends on three key factors.

The first of these is what is called 'international mobilization': media coverage, political influence, the support of public opinion and the involvement of international institutions. It should be noted that not all people are equal in the face of such international reaction. The Kurds benefited from the 'bonus' of international attention following the Gulf War. The media 'rating' of millions of Somalis, who are currently at risk of immediate death and yet no longer represent a strategic factor on the international scene, is clearly lower than that of the Kurds.

The second factor is the accessibility of people to aid. The logistics depend on the geographic context: during the 1984 famine in Ethiopia, it was no easy matter to organize food aid on the high plateaux, where the transport infrastructure was inadequate. Security problems are becoming a central question today with regard to aid in crisis situations. The work of humanitarian organizations is too often hampered by fighting and the warring factions' intransigence.

The third element, implicit in the first two, concerns the finance that can be made available to assist populations in danger, depending on the interest that public opinion and the main donors bring to their problems.

It is currently estimated that there are more than 40 million displaced persons or refugees throughout the world. No matter what the cause of these population movements, they almost always concern people from poor countries seeking refuge in areas with limited resources: Somalia, Sudan, Ethiopia, Malawi, Bangladesh or Mauritania have a per capita gross national product of less than 500 dollars a year, and an annual infant mortality rate higher than 120 deaths for every thousand live births. It is therefore essential to help the host countries deal with this extra 'burden', but without turning the refugees into 'favoured' aid recipients compared to local people.

Aid programmes are essentially composed of 10 clearly defined activities: an initial quick evaluation, the setting up of an epidemiological surveillance system and, in parallel, mass vaccination against measles, the supply of water, food and shelter, organized efforts to control diarrhoea-related illnesses, the training of health assistants and the provision of medical care based on standardized therapeutic techniques and above all the coordination of the various personnel involved.

Identifying health priorities depends on the collection of four types of information: the background to the displacement of the people concerned, a description of them, a calculation of the risk factors related to the main diseases and defining requirements in terms of human and material resources.

The background

The historical background can help in understanding, and sometimes in anticipating, the state of health of the refugees. This information, often anecdotal and difficult to evaluate, is obtained by interviews with the traditional, political or religious leaders. They define geographical origin, the social and ethnic composition of the group, the route taken, its length and, if possible, the death rate during the journey. The Somali refugees now crossing the Kenyan border at the rate of 500–1000 people a day settle in the Ifo camps after walking hundreds of kilometres. Mostly nomads, they have lost their herds and several members of their family, victims both of pillaging and the total absence of food. In the interior of the country, among refugees in the coastal region of Merca, it was estimated in April 1992, on the basis of a cursory survey, that one quarter of all the children under five had died during the year.

Population structure

An analysis of the structure of the population remains a major factor in the initial evaluation. A breakdown of refugee figures, and a description of their distribution by age, are indispensable. The demographic figures can usually be obtained by a census as people arrive if, for example, they are immediately registered for general food distribution.

Information about age distribution makes it possible to identify those who suffered most during displacement. In 1988, the Dinka who gathered at El Meiram, fleeing the war and famine ravaging southern Sudan, included fewer than five per cent of children under five, instead of the 20 per cent expected. This type of analysis reveals the high price paid by children under five in such situations.

Principal illnesses

During the emergency phase following a deplacement, the five most frequent conditions which take the heaviest toll on the displaced are: measles, diarrhoea, acute respiratory infections, malaria and malnutrition.

Measles is the worst problem. In the developing countries, it is a serious illness which kills one in every 10 children affected. Displacement, promiscuity and poor hygiene in the camps encourage the emergence of formidable epidemics. In Mauritania, in the Tuareg refugee camps in Bassikunu and Aghor, a survey in May 1992 showed that 40 per cent of deaths among children since the beginning of the year were attributable to measles, due to insufficient vaccination. The mass vacination of children up to the age of 15 should always be a top priority.

Diarrhoea is also a frequent cause of death. Each incidence exposes children to risk of death from acute dehydration. The swift installation of oral rehydration centres, spread throughout the reception area, helps to decrease the mortality rates associated with this condition. Population displacement often takes place in an area where cholera is still endemic and represents a major risk of epidemic. The seriousness of an epidemic can be gauged from the 'rate of attack', which is shown by the correlation between the number of cases and the total population concerned over a specific period of time. The rates of attack of diarrhoea recorded among the Mozambican refugees in Malawi from 1988 to 1991 varied between less than one per cent to more than six per cent. Where hundreds of thousands of refugees are concerned, the task of coping with such an epidemic requires major resources. Unless urgent therapeutic measures are taken, the number of deaths from cholera can reach up to half the reported cases. The setting up of a detection system, and of immediate rehydration, helps to reduce the death rate to an acceptable minimum level. In Malawi, during the period under consideration, mortality varied from zero to 10 per cent, depending on the reception site.

Respiratory infections, malaria and other common diseases must be dealt with in a series of health-care centres, with good coordination between them. A reasonable and limited list of essential medicines, adapted to the environment, should cover the great majority of illnesses, almost all of which can be cured with a simple therapeutic arsenal.

Nutrition-related diseases have a particular importance as population displacements are very often the cause – or the consequence – of a food shortage. The nutritional evaluation is therefore a key element in the initial survey. It is often made on the basis of a sample nutritional survey, either targeted or by random choice among a repre-sentative sample of the population. Malnutrition related to a protein-energy deficiency is measured by calculating the percentage of malnourished children among those aged under five. Normally, in the context of an emergency, the indicator used is the corre-lation between the weight and the height of the child compared to standard charts. The percentage of malnutrition is expressed in correlation to the 'norm'. By this method, an official inquiry in the Ifo refugee camp in May 1992 showed a malnutrition rate of more than 40 per cent, which led to the immediate opening of many intensive feeding centres. This nutritional evaluation allows an estimate of the number of children who should benefit from specific programmes because they face a high mortality risk.

Nutritional surveys are not the only means of supervising the food needs of a population. During the months following the installation of a camp, maximum attention must be given to the basic food ration. This should be a daily minimum of 2000 calories per person. If this level of distribution can be maintained, the number of people requiring intensive feeding will considerably decrease, as will the death rate.

What appears to be an adequate calorie ration can still be short on vitamins – which is often the case when food supplies are totally dependent on international aid. Epidemics of beriberi (caused by a shortage of vitamin B12) among the Cambodian refugees in Thailand, of scurvy (deficiency of vitamin C) among the Ethiopian refugees in Somalia, and of pellagra (niacin deficiency) among the Mozambicans in Malawi, all bear witness to the inadequacy of this aid in the long term. Only a system of supervising the rations actually received by the refugees, and of planning their needs, can help to avoid disasters such as the 18,000 cases of pellagra among the Mozambican refugees in Malawi in 1990.

Epidemiological surveillance is a tool for measuring, and following up on, a population's state of health. It gives quantified information to those in charge and should be put in place from the beginning. It depends on daily collection of a number of health indicator statistics and a weekly, and then monthly, analysis of these. This targeted survey should only be concerned with diseases, or other health incidents which can be the object of prevention or effective cure.

Among the health indicators to watch out for as from the emergency phase, the daily mortality rate represents the most useful information. It is most often expressed as the number of deaths – all causes included together – per 10,000 people per day. In 1988, in Sudan, the death rate among the Dinka reached almost 40 per 10,000 per day. Between June and October 1988, more than a quarter of the population died. Death rate statistics broken down into causes distinguish the part played by each illness and help in determining priorities.

One of the objectives of epidemiological surveillance is to give warning when an epidemic arises. Only early intervention can reduce mortality rates. This could take the form of detection and rapid treatment in the case of cholera, mass vaccination against meningitis A or B, or against measles. Such supervision also makes it possible to follow the trends of the principal illnesses and to measure the impact of the health programmes under way. High death rates usually continue for a few weeks. Their decrease and a return to rates comparable with those in the country of origin of the people concerned, and of the host country, marks the beginning of the 'post-emergency' phase, or the phase of installation of the refugees.

Needs and resources

Information which must be gathered during the first days of the emergency phase includes the possibilities and conditions for shelter, and for supplying water and food.

The type of environment affects the risk of diverse, potentially epidemic, diseases – measles, meningitis, typhoid, infectious diarrhoea and cholera, which occur more frequently and more severely where there is a high density of population.

Supply of drinking water is an absolute priority. The health indicator is here expressed in the number of litres of drinking water available per person per day – 20 litres is considered necessary. Plastic containers are usually used and supplies provided by tankers until wells are bored. Transport possibilities, knowledge of the climate and the passability of roads, all affect the supply of water and associated diseases. The quality of the water is checked by equipment which is easy to use.

Coordination of the work of the different aid agencies remains the principal element regarding aid in an emergency situation. The UNHCR plays the paramount role in the coordination of often delicate situations, where political and diplomatic questions are mixed in with logistic and technical problems.

The definition and organization of tasks require different categories of personnel: public health doctors, water engineers, logisticians and administrators. Particular attention must be paid to the training of local personnel (community health assistants and nurses). Such training not only shares knowledge but also helps the refugees to take responsibility for some of their health problems.

Methods of caring for displaced populations are now well systematized. Some emergency medical aid organizations which have suitable logistic resources have acquired the professionalism indispensable to this type of operation. The coordination of the different partners in an emergency operation plays an essential role in its success. But the major preoccupation of these organizations remains access to victims, knowing that the arrival of help depends first of all on an unpredictable international reaction.

Jean Rigal

POPULATION EXPLOSION: MYTHS AND REALITIES

As the first section of this report shows, the world's major crises are more the result of human passions than the whims of Nature. War and tyranny with their aftermath of violence, exodus and social turmoil are the main modern vectors of famine and epidemics. They are also the major roadblocks in the fight against poverty. With unfailing genius throughout history, humans have always found the resources and techniques, not only for saving life, but for inflicting death as well. But aid, especially in the form of medicine and food, is more and more frequently blamed for the demographic consequences it creates. With 'death control' techniques, as the French economist Alfred Sauvy calls them, more easily applicable than 'birth control' techniques, the world's population is artificially increasing. This leads to the accusation that by removing the link between the number of people and available resources, aid aggravates rather than relieves shortages. Are we not actually committing a wicked act by diminishing the human toll of wars and famines – traditional 'regulators' of global population – under the cover of generosity? Are the people who receive aid not condemned to a short life of poverty, while their countrymen's lives are only made worse and, beyond them, their contemporaries in general?

Everyone, including charity relief workers, has asked themselves such questions, which are only the vaguely rehashed ideas expounded by Malthus in his *An Essay on the Principle of Population*. In a world with limited resources, population, explained Malthus, tends to increase faster than the food supply unless obstacles get in the way to prevent it. It is just these obstacles – Malthus defined them as destroyers: poverty, famine and war – that aid attacks, especially humanitarian aid. It is by reducing the effects of these 'obstacles' – since it is clear that they eliminate neither misery nor war but attenuate their human consequences – that aid seems to fulfil the Malthusian prophesy, i.e. a population that increases by 100 per cent every 25 years is doomed to famine.

Used for a long time for national consumption, demographic theories and forecasts became universal again at the end of the 1950s when the Third World emerged as a political entity. The general optimism of the 1960s – founded on the strong growth of some and the conviction that the others, once independent, would join in the growth – showed absolute faith in the worldwide process of 'modernization'. This left little room for population and environmental questions. In fact miracles were long in coming, and scepticism carried the day. Theoretical development models flourished, and Malthusian ideas returned with a vengeance, as in the 1965 speech by Mr. Sen, then director general of the FAO, as a famine in Asia was beginning to rear its ugly head, when he addressed the UN Population Commission. Breaking with the established agenda, he spoke in these terms. 'We at the FAO have not succeeded in providing humankind with enough food. It is now up to you, the Population Commission, to reduce their number.' Supplanting the 'yellow peril' concept, the 'P bomb' ('P' for population) appeared. Demography exploded, and pictures of poverty-stricken crowds became synonymous with the Third World, while the industrialized countries harboured a growing fear of their own decline, even of a sort of implosion. It was in 1969 that the UN created its agency specializing in population, the UNFPA, followed in 1972 by its counterpart for the environment, the UNEP. The demographic spectre spread throughout the world and became well implanted by the 1980s. Africa, the last bastion against this thrust, found a rational explanation for its failure in developmental matters that its leaders gladly imputed to the too-rapid growth of their populations. It was in such a context that the new aid paradigm emerged: population growth aggravates underdevelopment and poverty which then cause an increase in migratory flows towards the developed countries. As a result, development aid, which now systematically includes a 'family planning' clause supporting the new population policies of the Third World, is thought to be the only way to hold back the migratory tidal wave that threatens to submerge the developed countries.

It was also during the 1980s that concern over ecology emerged. Possible irreversible damage to nature was added to demographic worries. It was mainly technological disasters that gave rise to this new awareness: nuclear accidents as at Chernobyl and Three Mile Island, oils spills, the chemical accidents at Seveso, Bhopal and Mexico City, as well as the greenhouse effect and the destruction of the ozone layer. The Frankenstein syndrome was reactivated; the creature had got away from its master again, and, having lost control of the forces we brought into the world, we were on a collision course with our own destruction. Everything is set for the meeting of the two phenomena. Because of our desire to master technology and the growing demographic burden, humankind has been gradually reduced to a universal predator. This explains, at least in part, why inhumane, forced population transfers like those carried out in Ethiopia during the famines of 1984 and 1985 were greeted understandingly by public opinion, international organizations and non-governmental organizations. There was also the success of the wonderful media and political extravaganza staged by Reagan and Gorbachev when they orchestrated the saving of two ice-bound whales in 1988 while at the same moment tens of thousands of people were starving to death amid general indifference.

Over the years the idea has come to be accepted that population growth simultaneously increases poverty and accelerates the deterioration of the environment, the end result of which can only be a migratory invasion of the industrialized countries. The idea has been considerably strengthened by the growing influence of the green movement.

While no one doubts the reality of demographic problems or the importance of protecting the environment from increasingly serious attacks, it is also legitimate to question the equation that is largely agreed upon today, i.e. population growth = deterioration of the environment = increase of poverty = increase of migrating hordes. In other words, the questions to be asked are of two kinds. By how much are demographics really exploding? And is the population element decisive in development, environment and migrations? Contrary to generally accepted ideas, neither of these questions can be answered simply and clearly.

The demographic explosion is mostly behind us, even if its effects are still being felt. Opposed to the Malthusian theory of geometric population growth is the 'demographic transition' theory, now largely confirmed by experience, in which the passage from one balanced phase to another takes place. The 'archaic' phase, typified by high rates of mortality and fertility, gives way, in a period of demographic transition, to a 'modern' phase typified by low rates of mortality and fertility. In the transitional phase mortality diminishes earlier than fertility, and population growth follows a 'bell' curve that accelerates rapidly to a pinnacle, then slows back down. It is the temporary gap between the two basic demographic parameters that causes the big surge in population growth. The coefficient by which the population is multiplied during the transition – called a transitional multiplier – is naturally a function of the width and duration of this gap. The population growth rate for Asia and Latin America reached a maximum in the 1960s, while Africa will reach it only at the beginning of the next century, thereby reattaining the percentage of the world's population that it had toward 1650, i.e. 20 per cent. Will Africa be the exception to what seems to be a general rule of evolution? The flimsiness of available statistical data for Africa leaves almost all hypotheses open. There is little doubt that the accelerating growth phase is more intense and longer than anywhere else, but the recent and reliable census in Nigeria lends weight to the 'anti-disaster' camp. Estimates had been put as high as 120 million people in Nigeria, but it has been shown that in fact there are only 90 million, thereby lowering the number of inhabitants of Africa's most populous country by nearly 30 per cent and moving the growth rate from the African average three per cent to 2.2 per cent, which is the Latin American average. Are the total population figures and the growth rates overestimated for the whole African continent? If so, are they in the same proportion as in Nigeria? No one today can answer these questions with certainty.

Information is, however, more reliable in the rest of the world and, because of the inertia of demographic data, it allows us to make some interesting forecasts. According to the United Nations and the World Bank, the world will count 8.5 billion inhabitants by 2025, 80 per cent of whom will be in countries with low fertility rates, and 20 per cent, or 1.7 billion people, in countries with high fertility rates. The large Asian and Latin American countries of the Third World will have moved into the first category with the second being composed essentially of sub-Saharan Africa and part of the Near East. Obviously, this does not represent exponential growth throughout the Third World but a much more limited figure. It is on this specific section of the world's population that planning efforts and demographic control should be concentrated.

Population pressure is only one of the factors causing the deterioration of the environment. Deforestation, desertification, exhaustion of arable land and water resources and pollution of the urban centres are the main environmental problems observed in the Third World. There too, links with demographic pressure are real but complicated and finely shaded. In fact, there are six broad categories of closely associated factors that lead to environmental deterioration. The three main factors are population growth, laws on land ownership and drift from the land. The three other factors of highly variable importance according to country and region are the kind of agricultural development and the abuse of certain lands because of economic pressure from the developed countries, the industrialization imperative and the adoption of high energy-consumption habits.

In regions where the traditional systems of crop rotation and fallowing are practised, the requirements of increasing agricultural production lead to a reduction, even outright suppression, of fallow periods and gradual exhaustion of the soil. A direct consequence of demographic pressure, the cultivation of mediocre, fragile, rapidly exhausted soil puts farmers in a situation that rapidly becomes desperate. Likewise, an increase in livestock – especially due to an improvement in care – produces devastating over-grazing that is often facilitated by the wildcat sinking of wells. The increasing population is evidently central to this process, but it should nonetheless be considered in the context of stagnating agricultural techniques for which Third World governments are largely to blame. Even when soil quality allows – which is not always the case – changing to intensive farming with fertilizers, deep ploughing and specially selected seeds is in fact an outright adventure for the farmer who has to overcome the multiple bureaucratic and political obstacles that keep him from obtaining acceptable credit conditions, seeds and the necessary nitrates. Bureaucratic centralization and the lack of interest in agricultural development have combined to muzzle, even break, the transitional process from extensively agrarian cultivation, which is extremely predatory but well adapted to wide open spaces, to more intensive farming that by now has become indispensable.

Another major element repsonsible for environmental deterioration in the Third World, especially in Africa, is the system of land ownership. Land and water access was formerly strictly regulated by traditional laws by imposing tribal limitations, duties, maintenance work of wells or periods of fallowing. Under pressure from governments and international development agencies – as determined to modernize as they are incoherent – the structure of land ownership has become unstable. In the absence of any apparent owner – either individual or collective – the traditional restrictions have vanished, and with them, any form of regulation. Over-grazing, the sanding up of wells, exhaustion of the thin mantle of Sahelian plant life and an increasingly encroaching desert have ensued. Rather than being a climatic and demographic problem, desertification is a social and political problem that occurs in the Ardèche region of France as well as the Sahel.

It seems in fact that for any given economic activity the damage caused to the environment is the result of three factors: population size, the level of consumption per head and the technology used. This latter factor should be considered in all its complexity, technology itself being the result of other factors that are hard to quantify, as we have seen for agricultural techniques. Quantitative studies show, however, that population pressure is not primary in environmental damage.

Agricultural production, a basis for economic development, has increased more rapidly in the world than the population, contrary to the forecasts of the disaster aficionados in the 1960s. It must be emphasized that only Africa is the exception. Agricultural production there is advancing twice as slowly as in the rest of the world and more slowly than the population, making Africa further dependent on international aid. This means that the popular picture of economic progress being 'eaten' by a devouring birth rate is an exception. And even here it should be noted that behind these statistics, which ignore individual situations, countries with high demographic growth like Ruanda, Kenya and Nigeria have managed very honourable economic performances. We might recall that 30 years ago India with its 300 million people was written off by experts as heading inevitably towards poverty and famine. Its fertile deltas were overworked, its countryside overpopulated. Whatever injustices the country may harbour, at least modern-day India produces enough crops to feed its 850 million inhabitants, thereby demonstrating what certain demographers claim, i.e. population growth can also be a 'catalyst for innovation', sometimes even a prerequisite for technical progress. Observed in several regions of the world, although not on a global scale, the mechanism is simple: increase of population density leads to a required growth in productivity, which in turn leads to a general development of production facilities. Here it is the people who benefit from technical progress and political evolution.

As for floods of immigrants which balanced development, reasonable demographic growth and integration of the world market are meant to calm, they have now become part of our contemporary world, independent of these other variables. On the one hand the main migratory nations of Africa are noticeably former colonies, which have maintained a very special relationship, independent of demographic density, with their former colonial power. For example the thinly populated countries of West Africa

149

are, along with Algeria, the main exporters of manpower towards France. If it is not population pressure, it is said, then development will surely help to curb migrations – fear is again coming to the rescue of development aid. The results, however, cannot stand up to analysis, for as Jean-François Bayart notes for Africa, 'a more integrated world economy will more than likely provoke the transfer of a lot of sub-Saharan manpower to the great western cities', as the creation of a national French market in the 19th century encouraged a lot of workers to leave their native Brittany and Auvergne for Paris. This in fact can be seen in Central America where the strongest migratory pressure on the United States comes from the most dynamic of the Central American countries like Colombia and El Salvador. Supposing by some miracle that development aid really leads to development (which, until now, has never been the case), the flow of migratory workers would still not be turned around.

For ideological or opportunistic reasons – or merely because it's stylish – population growth is blamed as the essential trigger of the cycle of economic failure and destruction of the environment. The ageing West loves to turn into an ideology its fear of a world it perceives as threatening, without even trying to find realistic arguments and facts for defending this perception. The governments of numerous Third World countries, after having so long rejected, on principle, the very idea that demographic increase could be problematic, now understand the advantages they can derive from this fear: a kind of customs clearance of their political and economic bad habits and a new boost for the guaranteed-income economy that a certain number of them have now set up. Backed by such total consensus, how could the idea not be successful? While rejecting the reverse dogmatism of 'demographic optimism', it is essential to resituate demographic growth, the problems it leads to and the dynamic it contains. After all it is the passions, aberrations and selfishness of humans, no matter what their numbers, that are and will always be at the root of disasters.

Rony Brauman

The main bibliographical source for this article is 'Relations entre Demographie et Environnement', D. Tabutin and E. Thitges, in *Tiers Monde*, April–June, 1992.

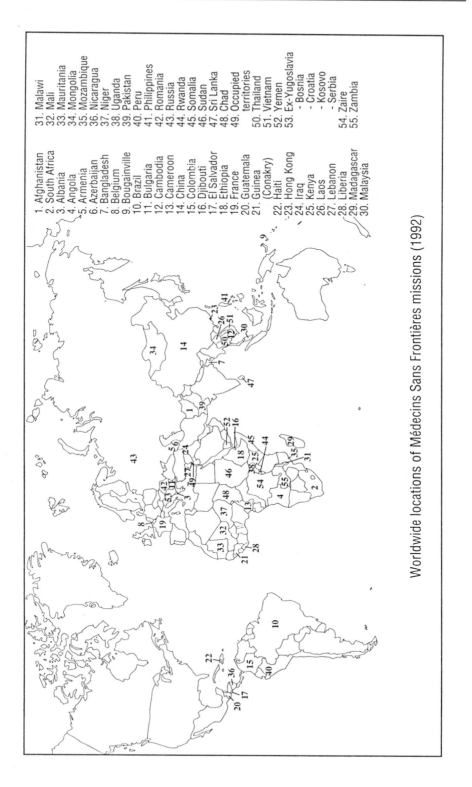

Worldwide locations of Médecins Sans Frontières missions (1992)

1. Afghanistan
2. South Africa
3. Albania
4. Angola
5. Armenia
6. Azerbaijan
7. Bangladesh
8. Belgium
9. Bougainville
10. Brazil
11. Bulgaria
12. Cambodia
13. Cameroon
14. China
15. Colombia
16. Djibouti
17. El Salvador
18. Ethiopia
19. France
20. Guatemala
21. Guinea
    (Conakry)
22. Haiti
23. Hong Kong
24. Iraq
25. Kenya
26. Laos
27. Lebanon
28. Liberia
29. Madagascar
30. Malaysia
31. Malawi
32. Mali
33. Mauritania
34. Mongolia
35. Mozambique
36. Nicaragua
37. Niger
38. Uganda
39. Pakistan
40. Peru
41. Philippines
42. Romania
43. Russia
44. Rwanda
45. Somalia
46. Sudan
47. Sri Lanka
48. Chad
49. Occupied
    territories
50. Thailand
51. Vietnam
52. Yemen
53. Ex-Yugoslavia
    - Bosnia
    - Croatia
    - Kosovo
    - Serbia
54. Zaire
55. Zambia

Medecins sans frontieres

MSF is a private, non-profit, international organization, whose objective is to provide medical aid to populations in crisis, without discrimination.

The organization relies on volunteer health professionals and is independent of all States or institutions, as well as of all political, economic or religious influences.

MSF was established in 1971 by doctors determined to offer emergency assistance wherever wars and man-made disasters occur in the world. Its guiding principles are laid down in a charter to which all members of the organization subscribe.

During 20 years of relief work around the world, MSF has gained a wide range of expertise, tested techniques and strategies of intervention that allow it to pool rapidly the logistics and human resources necessary to provide efficient aid.

Largely supported by private donors, the organization is able to maintain great interventional flexibility and total independence in its choice of operations. Moreover, in bearing witness to violations of basic humanitarian principles and denouncing them publicly, MSF volunteers implement a vital part of their humanitarian commitment.

The international MSF network is made up of operational sections and delegate offices in 12 countries. An International Office, based in Brussels, is responsible for liaising with international organizations.

This year, more than 2,000 Médecins Sans Frontières, of 45 different nationalities, worked in 58 countries. MSF spends 85 per cent of its total budget, 127 million ECU, on field operations.

To receive information about Médecins Sans Frontières, and to support its actions, please complete the coupon below and return it to the most appropriate address.

Operational sections:

Belgium
Artsen Zonder Grenzen
Médecins Sans Frontières
24 rue Deschampheleer
1080 BRUSSELS

Spain
Medicos Sin Fronteras
Avda Portal del Angel no.1,1
08002 BARCELONA

France
Médecins Sans Frontières
8 rue Saint-Sabin
75011 PARIS

Greece
Giatri Horis Synora
11A rue Paioniou
104 40 ATHENS

Luxembourg
Médecins Sans Frontières
110 av. Gaston Diderich
L-1420 LUXEMBOURG

The Netherlands
Artsen Zonder Grenzen
Postbus 10014
1001 EA AMSTERDAM

Switzerland
Médecins Sans Frontières
1 Clos de la Fonderie
1227 CAROUGES/GENEVA

Offices and representatives:

Australia
Doctors Without Borders
24 Angus Avenue
EPPING NSW 2121

Canada
Doctors Without Borders
56 The Esplanade, Suite 202
TORONTO, ONTARIO M5E 1A7

United States
Doctors Without Borders
30 Rockefeller Plaza, Suite 5425
NEW YORK, NY 10112

1999 Avenue of the Stars, Suite 500
LOS ANGELES, CA 90067

United Kingdom
Médecins Sans Frontières
3–4 St Andrews Hill
LONDON EC4V 5BY

Italy
Medici Senza Frontiere
1 via Galuzzi
00152 ROME

International Secretariat

Médecins Sans Frontières International
209 bd Léopold II
1080 BRUSSELS

I should like to support the work of Médecins Sans Frontières:

☐ Please send me further information
☐ I enclose a donation of ....

Name...
Address..
....
Town/Country...